THE DEEPER CAUSES
OF THE WAR
AND ITS ISSUES

A COLLECTION OF ADDRESSES GIVEN
UNDER THE AUSPICES OF THE
BRITISH INSTITUTE OF PHILOSOPHY
IN THE
ASSEMBLY HALL OF THE ROYAL
EMPIRE SOCIETY, LONDON

THE DEEPER CAUSES OF THE WAR AND ITS ISSUES

by

PROFESSOR
W. G. S. Adams

PROFESSOR
Gilbert Murray

THE RT. HON.
Viscount Samuel

THE VERY REV.
W. R. Matthews

Sir Richard Livingstone

Sir Richard Gregory

PROFESSOR
Ernest Barker

Sir William Beveridge

WITH A FOREWORD BY THE EDITOR
Sydney Ernest Hooper

Essay Index Reprint Series

BOOKS FOR LIBRARIES PRESS
FREEPORT, NEW YORK

First Published 1940
Reprinted 1970

STANDARD BOOK NUMBER:
8369-1517-8

LIBRARY OF CONGRESS CATALOG CARD NUMBER:
72-107715

PRINTED IN THE UNITED STATES OF AMERICA

FOREWORD

In early times man's life, owing to its impotence in dealing with a callous Nature, was brief and brutish. In our own time, the very power over Nature in the air, on the land, on the sea and under the sea, which natural science has put into man's hands, threatens human civilisation with disaster. Two groups of people in Europe, roughly numbering eighty millions each, now confront one another, organised to the last degree in industry and in the fighting services for mutual destruction. And this after many centuries of Christianity in the Western world and more recently of widespread education among all classes. What conclusion are we to come to in our reflection upon the tragic history of man? Is his case hopeless or can he yet be redeemed?

Nature, in producing many races with different languages, religions and social traditions, has set man a great task in the creation of order in the human world. There is certainly no pre-established harmony in respect of the diversities which characterise the human species. Moreover, the migrations and movements of peoples in Europe, before and during recorded history, took place with blind disregard of the many and great problems their promiscuous driftings and settlements were setting for future ages. With the passage of time, these peoples have developed strong national consciousnesses with

The Deeper Causes of the War

traditions and ambitions which often clash with one another, causing widespread restlessness among all, and in the weaker nations evoking profound fear of aggression from the strong.

At the end of the last war it was hoped that the nations of Europe had at length discovered a way by which they could live peaceably together, and a method of settling differences without resort to force. But, alas, after twenty years the high hopes set upon the League of Nations have been blasted, and Europe is again in travail. The terrible sacrifices of human life and treasure in the years 1914–18 appear to have been in vain.

It is not surprising, then, that the dread doubt whether man is equal to the task of maintaining a complex civilisation should be openly expressed by a few leading publicists and be secretly entertained in the minds of many thoughtful people. We seem to be faced with this question: Must Europe for ever be a battle-ground of warring nations, or is it possible by good will and common sense to establish an order which will satisfy the needs of the various nations and thus provide an atmosphere of freedom in which individuals may realise their potentialities for happiness and goodness?

A time has now been reached in human history when the ordinary European has come to regard war as a very great evil which threatens the continuance of civilised life. National governments, however, are so influenced by ambitions (sometimes reasonable and sometimes pernicious) or else are obsessed by fear of aggression,

Foreword

that conflicts of policy are as common as ever they were, and war ever lies in wait round the corner. In our own day, it has ceased to lie in wait, and has sprung upon us once more in all its fury. What the world will be like when the grim struggle is over, no one can foresee. Clearly a crisis has been reached, and unless it is possible to avert the grave danger that threatens the civilisation that Europe has painfully built up, moral and economic ruin will assuredly overtake us. Is there a way out of the impasse? Can Europe be changed from being a continent of irreconcilable warring peoples into a commonwealth of nations, united by co-operation in a constructive effort to achieve dignity, security and prosperity for each and all?

It was questions such as these that led The British Institute of Philosophy to arrange the series of addresses delivered during the past winter and now collected together in this book. They are designed to answer such questions as far as it is possible to do this. Convinced that many thoughtful minds were deeply troubled by the recurring conflicts of the great nations of Europe, it was decided to invite men eminent in different departments of human thought to give addresses on *The Deeper Causes of the War and its Issues*. Each speaker has done his best to probe to the bottom of the present war and to suggest a remedy for the unhappy discords in Europe. Science, Philosophy, Religion, History have had their say. The question in debate is a wide and comprehensive one. It is nothing less than whether man is capable of maintaining (let alone of advancing) the civilisation he has built up. Man at his best aspires to the heights, but he is not unaware of the depths from which he has sprung. Is he great enough for the task allotted to him by Nature? Is his late-born moral consciousness strong enough to take control of the future history of nations in their relations with one another, or is he destined for ever to be the tragic victim of internecine conflict? It is for the reader to judge of the whole matter after reading and pondering what has been written in the following pages.

The Council of The British Institute of Philosophy wishes to thank the contributors to this volume for their generosity in giving their addresses as a free gift to the Institute; and to the publishers for making the proposal to have them issued in this form and for the care they have taken in carrying the proposal into execution.

SYDNEY E. HOOPER

March 1940

CONTENTS

		PAGE
	FOREWORD	7
I.	RIGHTS AND VALUES by Professor W. G. S. Adams, C.H., D.C.L.	13
II.	HERD INSTINCT: FOR GOOD AND EVIL by Professor Gilbert Murray, D.C.L., D.LITT., F.B.A.	28
III.	SOWING AND REAPING by the Rt. Hon. Viscount Samuel, G.C.B., G.B.E., HON.D.C.L.	56
IV.	THE WAR AND THE CRISIS FOR THE SPIRIT OF MAN by the Very Rev. W. R. Matthews, K.C.V.O., D.D., D.LIT.	76
V.	THE CRISIS OF CIVILISATION by Sir Richard Livingstone, D.LITT., LL.D.	94
VI.	SCIENCE AND HUMANE VALUES by Sir Richard Gregory, BART., F.R.S.	116
VII.	THE PROBLEM OF AN ORDER OF EUROPE by Professor Ernest Barker, LL.D., LITT.D.	138
VIII.	PEACE BY FEDERATION? by Sir William Beveridge, K.C.B., B.C.L., F.B.A.	156

I

RIGHTS AND VALUES*

by

Professor W. G. S. Adams
C.H., D.C.L.

"The deeper causes of the war and the issues involved" is a subject which we have to try and think about in clear and simple language. Much that can be said is familiar to us, but the fact that it is familiar is not a reason why we should not reconsider and re-estimate time and again this question. We need to keep our thoughts clear and to carry on the policy of testing what we think in the light of our own and others' experience.

It is, as I understand, the intention not to divide up the subject into separate aspects of this very large question, but rather to leave each of us free to express that which he feels most deeply on the subject, and to allow emphasis on any particular line of thought to be left to the individual. If, as may well be, there is considerable convergence in the emphasis, that is in itself some testimony to real causes and effects.

Such a time as the present is a testing time of values. All of us, whether or not we give much expression to

The Deeper Causes of the War

our inmost thoughts, are searching our own minds, and most of us are interested in what our fellows are thinking because we know that thought is very much the true essence of action and that the community of our thoughts is a measure of the unity of our effort. It is therefore not something unnecessary or unpractical to take time to think over and over again for ourselves why we are at war and what is at stake in the issues.

War is the defeat of civilisation. The world wished for and wishes for peace. War has come. Why? There was a hope for peace and a desire for peace—a deep world desire. There was a hope and a reasonable hope. The world has been advancing towards peace and despite the set-backs, disappointments and failures, the world is still marching towards peace. Let us never be despondent, still less defeated. As we look back and look around us there is reason for hope. The last great world war was to see the end of war. By far the greatest effort ever made to end war was the establishment of a solemn covenant to end war, and this was followed by other efforts to the same end. The Covenant of the League of Nations and the building of the machinery and administration of the League was a deliberately planned and sustained effort to establish the rule of peace. The Kellog Pact was another expression of the will of the nations to peace. These efforts have for the present failed and the world is facing again the cruel arbitrament of war. But the Covenant of the League, the Kellog Pact, and many other achievements, especially

Rights and Values

in the international provision for arbitration and the solution of disputes between nations, are all steppingstones on the way to peace. The work will go forward despite the interruption of war. There is reason for encouragement in this progress in the pursuit of peace.

Let us look around in another way. Who of us cannot but recognise that progress has been made in securing, not only within great States but in the relations between groups of States, a basis of peaceful progress? It is a reasonable claim that in the two great American continents the basis of peace has been well laid and tested. Within the British Commonwealth, despite the unrests and even civil wars, or threats thereof, who can doubt that peace has been progressively secured? And between these two great Commonwealths, the American and the British, war to-day or in the future is unthinkable. That is a great step towards world peace. But who of us also does not feel that between the British Commonwealth and the French Republic, after our common sacrifices, war is unthinkable? So, too, it is with the Scandinavian and many other States. We can all follow up this train of thought and realise that there is an increasing group of States between whom, to-day and in the future, war is unthinkable. Even despite this war do we not agree that the chance of peace was more in the balance than before? There was a hope at least that peace, permanent peace, might be safeguarded. Having thus far advanced, why war?

We ask ourselves the question, and stubbornly we

The Deeper Causes of the War

must go on asking ourselves the question—"What are the causes of war?" For this war is but an example and the result of all those causes which lead to war. The causes of war have grown deeper and more serious. No nation to-day goes lightly to war, for not only the nations at war but the nations at peace suffer from war far more than ever before. War is world-wide in its repercussions; neutrals as well as belligerents suffer. The few that gain something are few, against the many that lose much—it may be everything, or almost everything. We may put the question in another form—we may ask, "What are the deeper causes of peace?" The effort to probe down into the causes of war and peace is practical, and the need is urgent. If, as we believe, we have taken up arms for a just cause, then to know what are the deeper issues at stake for which we are fighting is of the greatest practical concern to us all. There has been much said and written about this war being a war of nerves. It is more truly a war of morale. It is a war, the issue of which depends on the strength, justice and truth of the conviction that we hold. The problem is not only to win the war but to win the peace. These two problems are one and indivisible. We shall be strong to endure the sufferings and sacrifices of war if we have the vision of true and secure peace. We have, therefore, to think deeply, to think steadily and continuously of the principles for which we are fighting; and to think deeply, steadily and continuously of the peace which can prevent the recurrence of war. It is the

Rights and Values

most serious challenge to thought and to action for every one of us.

But before we go further we must be critical, critical of ourselves before we are critical of others; we must see that there is not the beam in our own eye. We must be also constructive. We must be critical, and one of the best ways of being critical is by asking questions of ourselves. We know that lack of confidence between nations has been a cause of the present failure. Have we not our share of responsibility in this lack of confidence? Why is it that we are distrusted? Is there not some reason for this? Have we carried out our obligations and our trusteeship as we should have done? Have we tried to understand the mentality of those who have not felt and thought as we have? Have we been fair in our appreciation of their difficulties and their achievements? Have we discriminated and recognised what was positive and good in the systems which other countries have developed? Have we tried to weigh dispassionately their grievances?

The failure of collective security is not merely the failure to provide an armed sanction against aggression, it is also a failure collectively to recognise what was wrong in the *status quo*, and to see that we seriously endeavour to put it right. And have we not shown our weakness also in dealing with the provision in our own country for social security? We cannot keep apart, as two separate things, social policy and foreign policy. The one subtly but really affects the other. We have to

The Deeper Causes of the War

try and see ourselves as others see us. Has not war revealed to us already our social weakness and shortcomings? For example, to what thinking, honest mind has the experience of evacuation not brought serious reflections on our social order? If it is so at home, what about our relations to other nations and the consideration of the claims not only of those with whom we are at conflict, but of the people who are under our trusteeship? Have we had the moral and spiritual courage to put our better thought into action?

Let us be critical first of all of ourselves if we are to understand what others feel about us and to be understood by them. For the basis of lasting peace is mutual understanding, confidence and the evidence and proof of good will. It is not easy to say these things, but in trying to search out so deep-rooted a question as the causes of war let us see that our judgment is kept clear by patient, honest, fearless self-criticism. It is the whole way of life—its material provisions, its social order, its spiritual vigour—which is concerned.

But the end of criticism is action and construction. We have to plan anew, and not only to hold to what is good in the achievements, institutions and policies of the past, but to build a new way of life—a highway of life—which is broad and strong enough to carry us forward into a more secure and better future. We realise the immense advance and the beneficence of science. We know that it is within our grasp to reach a higher standard of well-being throughout the world.

Rights and Values

But we must see to it that in the foundations of the new order first things come first. The old definition that "the State comes into existence to make life possible, and continues to exist to make life good," is true of the world order as well as of the State. Unless there is security the good life is threatened, and all the culture and progress connected with it. Therefore we must see to it that we use the rich experience of the past, and that we add to it the measures which our new world calls for if we are to have security and freedom. We must keep this double purpose in mind: to be critical and to be constructive, in thinking again of the deeper causes which have led to the present war.

Now may I in a very brief way say one or two things before coming to the main causes that I wish to discuss. We realise that the series of acts of aggression in Asia, Africa and Europe, have prepared the way for this war; we realise that the peace of Versailles had in it provisions which must have been modified by agreement if there were to be lasting peace; we realise that the League of Nations, based on the Covenant, had to be loyally supported and courageously and impartially directed if it were to be effective; we realise that disarmament was a solemn treaty obligation not carried out by the States which were party to the agreement; we realise that social and economic distress, the lack of after-care which needs to follow war, made unrest and misery widespread; we realise that the highly protective and exclusive nationalism, the restrictions on trade and

The Deeper Causes of the War

intercourse, the lack of a world financial order, destroyed confidence and mutual helpfulness; we realise that all these and other factors have been causes which have contributed to the conflict which we are facing. These are all well known; they stare us in the face.

But while we have in our minds many incidents and factors which have helped to bring about the present war, let me try to set out three of the causes which seem to me to go deep down into the roots of our problem.

The first cause is the denial of the rights of man, the second is the disregard of the rule of law, and the third and the deepest cause is the decline of spiritual and moral values. These three causes are all related one to the other, part of one another, but it may help us to try and look at each in turn.

The challenge to the rights of man lies in the rise of the Power State. This is not something new in the world, but a manifestation of it has come again in our time and has put forth the claim of a theory of the State which is a challenge to what we hold most essential, and to what we are trying to practise; the view of the State as not resting upon power but as based upon the fundamental rights and needs of man, a moral State, as man is moral. The long process of civilisation has slowly but painfully secured what have been called "the rights of man," phrased in many different forms. "Life, Liberty, Property and the Pursuit of Happiness"—to take one classical expression; "Liberty, Equality, Fraternity"—to take another. But what we think of above all

Rights and Values

as the rights that give value to life are the right of freedom from arbitrary arrest and confinement, the right of freedom of speech, the right of combination and association whether it be in a trade-union or a church. Man is a social being and these rights are the very expression of his social nature. The State exists to make these and many other rights real. The Might State, the Power State, is a denial of rights so conceived. In it such rights as these flow only from the State and can be denied by the State whenever the interests of its rulers so decree. Freedom from arrest, freedom of speech, freedom of combination, none of these are rights which are recognised in the Power State. The Power State has its own great ideal. Let us not misrepresent it. "The community is everything; you are nothing" is what one sees written up in the halls where youth is trained in the Power State. It makes a great call for sacrifice and for the service of the community, but it is most easily perverted; it can most easily deny and destroy to the individual the very things which make the good life possible. The Power State denies to the individual the fundamental rights of man. The State is absolute and sovereign. And just as it asserts its authority over the individual, so it will acknowledge no supernational authority. It cannot surrender its sovereignty to any federation or union of mankind. It is an apotheosis of the State which threatens both the liberty of the individual and the existence of the Commonwealth of Nations. When this theory of the

The Deeper Causes of the War

Power State is linked with a theory of racial exclusiveness and superiority, a theory which, whatever its scientific superficiality and unsoundness, is highly aggressive and dynamic, we realise how grave a menace such a contribution is to the peace of the world.

Closely linked with this denial of rights is the second cause which I have named: the disregard of the rule of law. We think of the rule of law as an order within the State. It is the mark of a free State. All citizens are equal before the law, and the law is administered independently by judges who are not the instruments of the executive authority. Within the State the independence of the judiciary is a cardinal principle of the rule of law. But the conception of the rule of law is even more significant for the future of civilisation in the relations between States. Just as within the State the liberty of the individual depends upon the law and its impartial exercise, so the liberty of nations must more and more be subject to the rules and conventions of international law. The hope for the peace of society lies in this direction. No longer must a nation be in a position to commit an act of aggression simply in pursuit of its sovereign power. If there is to be a state of world society and not a state of potential war, we must substitute the rule of reason for the rule of force; and the rule of reason is the rule of law. We have to face clearly the choice which is offered to society of accepting and conforming to the authority of international law if we are not to have a state of international anarchy. The Covenant of the

Rights and Values

League, the Kellog Pact, and other treaties provided that before committing acts of aggression nations should submit their disputes to inquiry and conciliation. A further stage is reached when nations are ready unconditionally to submit not only to inquiry and conciliation but finally to arbitration. Then only will the rule of law be established. All nations must be prepared, if they are to have the hope of peace, to renounce their absolute sovereignty, to renounce the claim of national right above the supreme international right. Then and then alone will there be the rule of law. But the theory of the Power State stands directly across the path of such developments. It denies the right of any but the sovereign State to determine its vital interests and its honour. And this applies not only to the totalitarian States. Most States have been and are Power States in some measure. We have been so as well as others; we have to be ready to limit our national sovereignty by international control. The world has advanced a long way in the twentieth century towards this ideal—though progress has been rudely shaken. None the less the issue stands clear before us and before all nations. These are great, simple, almost self-evident things, but they need to be stated again and again, and to become part of the creed and political testament of every man and woman.

To fulfil the vital function of inquiry, conciliation and arbitration, society must maintain and extend the machinery of international control. Rules must have

The Deeper Causes of the War

their sanctions. Sanctions is a word with angry associations, and all the wisdom of the world will be needed to discover the way in which fulfilment and honouring of obligations can be maintained. But there is one thing to remember, the higher we get in the scale of social development, the more does progress depend upon consent and the honouring of obligations. Yet unless with consent there goes disarmament, there must be, under the international authority, power to execute judgment superior to the power of any individual State. It is the threat of the dominant Power State, whether that State be democratic or autocratic in its form of government, which is the menace to peace. The rule of law, established and honoured, is the bulwark of peace; but the disregard of international agreement and the denial of the rule of law is the way that leads to war.

This brings me to the third cause: the decline of moral and spiritual values. This is the deepest of all the causes. We are in an age of great materialism, good and bad. The spectacular achievements of science, the critical analysis of traditions and beliefs, the perplexity of the issues and events of life, all tend to an unrest and thus to an apathy in moral and spiritual values. These values are apt to be thrust back and submerged. Yet they are the true cement of social order and progress. The rights of man, the rule of law, and common moral and spiritual values bind the world together. The denial of them loosens the solidarity of human society. To-day the power of the machine is very great over the human

Rights and Values

mind; and it is not only the physical machine; it is the power of the social mechanism and of that greatest social machine, the State. When we get a State that seeks to centralise power and to extend its control so as to secure the maximum of power and the elimination of independent thought, then truly we are faced with a development of great gravity for the well-being of the community. When family life and loyalty is disrupted, when the independence of the Church and our spiritual liberties are suppressed, when the rights of labour—great social and economic rights—are subjected to the might of the State, then the very moral fibre on which the strength of individual and social life depends is weakened.

The advance of social justice in any State helps the life of other States and binds the world together. How much, too, a common measure of spiritual things deepens the life of humanity! If the gain of these things is so great, great also is the loss due to their neglect. Religion, with all the shortcomings which its institutional forms present, is, as the word itself connotes, the binding force which deepens the sense of duty to our neighbour and of responsibility and reverence to God. Man is a spiritual as well as a social being. It is in the anarchy of spiritual and moral values that much of the unrest and the danger of our modern world lies. Nothing can replace, nothing can give so fully, the sense of responsibility which true religion enjoins. It is therefore a call to all men and women who know the power of moral principle

The Deeper Causes of the War

and the value of spiritual life, to bear witness to their fundamental significance for the peace and happiness of society.

May I carry this line of thought a step further? In one sense the deeper causes of war are not far to seek. To use a familiar word—the root cause of war is sin. Ignorance, error, selfishness, these are the things which bring war. We all share in this responsibility—no nation is clear. The failure to live up to our moral and spiritual standards—the true guides of life, individual, national and international—has brought moral and spiritual scepticism and anarchy. Therein lies the real danger of modern society. The plain virtues which we know are the root of the decent life of everyone of us: keeping faith; respect for the weak; the true discharge of trusteeship instead of exploitation; the spirit of mutual helpfulness; these are the principles which must govern national and international policy if we are to have peace and good will. There is one morality for all—for the individual, for the nation, for the commonwealth of nations; and the final purpose of international order is to enable the individual anywhere to try and live the good life. The international order is necessary to the national order just as the national order is necessary to the good life of the individual. To-day one of the evil things is the neglect and in some cases the proscription of much that is our common heritage. It seems almost incredible that the great literature of the Hebrews and of the Christian writers should be in some countries proscribed.

Rights and Values

It is in the meeting of cultures, the enrichment of our civilisation with the best of that which is from the East, as well as carrying on the heritage of Greece and Rome, that we get a community of common ideals and common standards of value. But above all, in the things of the mind and the spirit we need freedom, philosophic freedom, freedom to think things together. We have to reaffirm the rights of man, the rule of law, and the supremacy of moral and spiritual values. That is the way of peace.

II

HERD INSTINCT: FOR GOOD AND EVIL

by

Professor Gilbert Murray
D.C.L., D.LITT., F.B.A.

I HAD prepared a quite harmless address for this Institute on an agreeable philosophical problem, when I was rather suddenly switched off on to the dismal subject which occupies the minds of all of us to-day. I turned back to 1914 to study the sort of things said at that time by myself and various friends of mine, by the Principal of Newnham, most objective of judges, by Andrew Bradley, lover of Germany and steeped in German philosophy, and others. Among them I found an essay of my own on "Herd Instinct and the War," which was, I remember, approved by Lord Bryce, but criticised by Professor Macdougall as laying too much stress on the bad side of Herd Instinct and not enough on the good. This set me thinking again, and the present paper is the result.

War, as everyone recognises, involves an inordinate stimulation of Herd Instinct in all its forms. In every war each side is sure to believe that its own Herd stands for the good cause and the opposing Herd for the evil.

Herd Instinct: For Good and Evil

And of course we must remember that, though sometimes both may be wrong, in some cases one of them is right.

The Prime Minister in his broadcast of September 3rd ended his appeal to the nation with these words: "It is the evil things that we are fighting against—brute force, bad faith, oppression and persecution; and against them I am certain that the right will prevail."

I am sure he meant what he said. The words were not the mere rhetoric of a peroration or the crude invective that belongs to times of war. Lord Halifax afterwards quoted the paragraph in a broadcast of his own, which he would not have done unless he believed that it was true. I myself listened critically, almost suspiciously, and certainly without any impulse of war-fever; and I also believe that it is true. We are fighting not merely against a dangerous rival and enemy who has for some time been working for our destruction, but against a widespread force of Evil which, if unchecked, will wreck all the hopes of civilisation and which stands condemned equally by the normal standards of enlightened thought and by those of every traditional religion.

Now are we all deceived by our over-stimulated Herd Instincts, or is this thesis of the Prime Minister's really true? Of course the Germans think otherwise. One can quote not merely the wild present-day Nazis, but their predecessors of twenty-five years ago. They expressed themselves in lively terms even then. I was sent in 1915 by a neutral friend a patriotic German poem, which was

The Deeper Causes of the War

said to be much admired in German evangelical circles. It began by explaining that the German cause was God's cause, and proceeded: "We have become the nation of wrath.... We accomplish the almighty will of God, and will vengefully wreak the demands of His righteousness on the godless, filled with sacred fury.... We are bound together like a scourge of punishment whose name is War. We flame like lightning. Our wounds blossom like rose-gardens at the gate of heaven. Thanks be to Thee, God Almighty! Thy wrathful awakening does away with our sins. As the iron in Thy hand we smite all our enemies on the cheekbone." Another poet, a clergyman, prays that the Germans may not fall into the temptation of carrying out the judgment of God's wrath with too great mildness.

Now we need not take much trouble to show that this poet was deceiving himself, but it is important for us to make sure, if we can, that we ourselves are not doing the same. The outlines of our case are obvious: I need not dwell on the extraordinary brutalities committed on the victims of the Nazis in Germany, brutalities accompanied by every element of meanness as well as of cruelty; on the treacherous and savage treatment of Poles and Czechs, the glorification of war and the horrible misleading of the young which constitutes Nazi education. More significant still, perhaps, are the doctrines preached by Nazi intellectuals, pouring scorn not only on normal Christian morals but on the sanctity of truth itself, which it is the first duty of their profession to defend.

Herd Instinct: For Good and Evil

The Minister of Education at the great Heidelberg conference announced Nazi emancipation from "the false idea of objectivity," and obedient to him the Professor of Philosophy at Heidelberg declared: "We do not know of or recognise truth for truth's sake or science for science's sake." "We will never approach history impartially," writes *Die Deutsche Schule*, "but as Germans." History is not to be true history but German history; even physics, we hear from one of the greatest Nazi scientists, Professor Stark, must henceforth be "German physics," since pure physics have a taint of Einstein and Judaism about them. Together with the rejection of truth goes a rejection of justice. The reverence for moral right is a thing that "belongs to bygone times":[1] a German youth should not bother about whether he is acting nobly or basely: the thing that matters is that he acts; or in Dr. Goebbels's authoritative words, "What matters is not who is right but who wins." Especially between nations is any moral law out of place. "It smacks," as a leading Nazi once told me, "of Marxist ideology." "The only good peace," writes Herr Hitler, is a "peace established by the victorious sword of a master nation" (*Mein Kampf*, p. 438).

To take one particular instance of the state of mind we call evil, a strangely effective contrast was drawn by an English newspaper between the letter of Rathenau's Jewish mother to the mother of his murderer and the

[1] A publication of the *Deutscher Philologenband*, quoted by Ernest Wichert at the University of Munich, April 16, 1935.

The Deeper Causes of the War

comment of the *Schwarze Korps* on the killing of Vom Rath by a Jew. Mathilde Rathenau wrote:

"In my unspeakable grief I stretch out my hand to you, most suffering of women. Tell your son that I forgive him in the name and spirit of the murdered man, as may God forgive him if before an earthly justice he makes a full and open confession and repents before the justice of Heaven. Had he known my son, the most noble that the earth has borne, he would sooner have turned the murderer's weapon on himself than on him. May these words give your soul peace."

The *Schwarze Korps* writes:

"We shall use our Jewish hostages in a systematic way, no matter how shocking some people find it. We shall use the principle proclaimed by the Jews—'an eye for an eye, and a tooth for a tooth.' But we shall take a thousand eyes for one eye, and a thousand teeth for one tooth."

We must remember that both statements came from Germans. But it is the second attitude, not the first, that is approved by the German Government.

Yes, the contrast is there. The Nazi movement in Germany does represent a definitely evil principle, a moral poison which for the last eight years or so has been running through the world corrupting civilisation, and deeply affecting other nations such as Japan and Italy.

How can this be so? We used to speak not merely of German science, philosophy and music; we used to speak of German honesty and kindliness, German

Herd Instinct: For Good and Evil

Sittlichkeit. We thought of the typical German family as artistic, well educated and well brought-up, and a model of the domestic virtues. We most of us have German friends who fulfil all these expectations, and are more sympathetic to us than most foreigners. What has happened to make so catastrophic a change?

That is one side of the problem. Let us face the other.

If we are to collect and scrutinise the moral history of nations, are we sure that our own record is so good that when the Prime Minister asks God to "defend the right," we can take for granted that "the right" means Britain?

I believe that in the present case we can. I think this nation does, in the present conflict, stand for a great moral principle and that Germany stands for an evil principle; but to explain why I dare pronounce a judgment of so brazen and philistine an appearance I must go back, as befits a speaker in this Institute, from politics to philosophy, or at least to group psychology.

In that complex process of selection for survival which is rather unfortunately called the struggle for life, Herd Instinct plays a momentous part, and in Herd Instinct there are always two principles involved, one Destructive and one Protective; Fighting Power as against enemies and outsiders, and mutual protection between members of the Herd itself. Both are necessary. The Herd will perish if its fighters cannot stand up against the enemy; it will perish if its men do not protect its women, if its women do not tend their young and care for the sick and wounded. Prince Kropotkin in his book *Mutual*

The Deeper Causes of the War

Help has shown how such Mutual Help is as important a force for survival as any form of contest with enemies. "Altruism," the care for "autrui," is as necessary an instinct to a tribe as "egoism." And one of the recognised marks of an advance of civilisation in any human herd is the gradual extension of the boundaries of the herd, so as to take inside the circle of friendliness and mutual help more and more of those who were previously *hostes*—strangers and therefore enemies.

Now while conscious of the dangers of self-deception, I venture to suggest that for Great Britain this second form, the peaceful and protective, through purely historical causes is, and must be, peculiarly strong. I would cite three causes in particular.

In the first place, our whole national character has been profoundly influenced by our long security. We have not been invaded by a foreign army since the reign of King John, and not successfully invaded since William the Conqueror. Contrast the position of France, invaded thrice in a lifetime, and faced perpetually by an enemy, stronger than herself, just across an imaginary frontier. Being accustomed to safety we do not easily believe in danger. We are quite stupid in our insensitiveness to danger. Consequently we are free from all those evil lessons that "terror teaches," lessons of hate, of suspicion, of violence, of intolerance. No doubt the anxieties of recent years have had their effect upon us; but still we are on the whole a singularly good-natured, tolerant people, moderate in our political controversies, and eager to

Herd Instinct: For Good and Evil

shake hands with old opponents after a fight. Think of the great popular welcomes given to the Boer generals and to Gandhi; the wide popularity even of Hindenburg. There is a second reason. We are not only a people dependent on sea-borne trade, whose prosperity is bound up with peace; we are also a great imperial Power and one which is no longer aggressive. We have of course been aggressive in the past, though not quite so much so as people ignorant of Indian and colonial history are inclined to think; but that belongs to the past. As General Hertzog said after the Imperial Conference of 1926: "I have been a life-long opponent of imperialism and have feared the Empire, but as a result of the Imperial Conference the old Empire no longer exists. All that remains is a free alliance of Great Britain and six Dominions co-operating as friends...." I need not labour the point. We have carried this principle of government by consent, of mutual co-operation based on good will, to a degree unparalleled, as far as I know, in previous history. In our relations with Egypt, with Iraq, with India, where the problem is extraordinarily difficult, we are encouraging the growth of independence just as we have done in the Dominions. But that is not all. The movement is not merely a negative withdrawal from claims for greater expansion, a withdrawal that might be natural in a "satiated" empire—if such a thing exists; it is a positive acceptance of responsibilities for the welfare of all whom we feel to belong to us. Long experience of Empire has taught Great Britain a sense of almost world-wide

The Deeper Causes of the War

responsibility. I remember noticing at the Assembly of the League of Nations that, whereas most nations made a sharp distinction between matters that touched their interests and matters which they did not care about, almost everything that went wrong in the world was the care of the British Empire. If there is slave raiding in Africa, if there is piracy in the Yellow Sea, if there is plague in China, if the pilgrim routes to Mecca are endangered, if the buoys in the Persian Gulf are badly placed, at once Great Britain is expected to attend to the matter, and Great Britain always accepts the responsibility. We agree that these things matter to us. Speaking in terms of Herd Instinct, this means that we have taken the great mass of human kind into the circle of our herd. They belong to us, and we to them. They are our friends; and we protect them.

You may notice how the very accusations made against British policy are in accord with this conception, and are in fact almost a testimonial. Almost no one accuses us of aggression. Certainly no small nation is afraid of attack by Great Britain. The complaint always is that we have not fulfilled various duties and responsibilities which we, and no other nations, are expected to fulfil. We failed to protect China, failed to protect Abyssinia, Czechoslovakia, Albania; how disgraceful! Our critics pour obloquy on us. We ourselves feel in different degrees ashamed. But no other nation is blamed, because no other nation was ever expected to do such things.

I must add a third consideration of a quite different

Herd Instinct: For Good and Evil

kind which also compels us to be prime champions for peace and the rule of law. I spoke of our long-established insular security. That, as we all know, has been very seriously diminished by the invention of the aeroplane; but our position as an Empire is in reality much more precarious than that single consideration would suggest. There are, in the world as a whole, certain well-known seeds of possible war or sources of discord; and it is curious to observe that practically all of these are to be found working inside the British Empire.

There is the possible war of colours; how long will the yellow or the brown races tolerate the general supremacy of the white? How long will even the black millions of Africa remain contentedly at times half-enslaved and at times gravely ill-treated, especially when the French have so obligingly taught them military drill and the use of modern weapons? There is the clash of civilisations—Christian, Moslem and Oriental. There is the world problem of emigration and the distribution of population. How long will the overcrowded nations, like Japan, China, India, Italy, Poland, contentedly remain choked with surplus population, while the owners of the vast empty territories all round the Pacific, such as Australia, Canada, and the U.S.A., deny—and for very weighty reasons deny—their people the right of entry?

If war should break out anywhere from one of these causes, it is the British Empire that would be struck first, or almost first; if a war of colour, the Empire rules brown and black men by the million, and is more intimately

The Deeper Causes of the War

involved with yellow China than any other European Power. She presents the contrast of white ruler and coloured subject on the greatest scale. If there is a war of civilisations, if Moslem ever rises against Christian, or Hindu against either, it is inside the Empire that the explosion will take place. If a war breaks out on the emigration question, the Empire contains to a high degree both the territories that demand emigration as a necessity of existence and the territories that will never admit immigrants. We are tied to the most disturbed of continents, Europe; to the most dangerous of oceans, the Pacific. We are interpenetrated by the most formidable of subject civilisations, Islam. We are the chief representative of the most hotly disputed of international principles, the rule of one race of men over another. The safety of the Empire, it seems to me, depends absolutely on the tranquillity and general welfare of the world.

Thus, if we claim that in the present struggle the cause of Britain represents the Right, or the Good of humanity, that does not mean that Englishmen are by nature specially unselfish or virtuous; it means that owing to historical causes it has come about that the chief interest and aim of the British Empire is wrapped up with the general good of the human race. Our care for peace, our desire for reconciliation, our faith in the ideal of the League of Nations, are neither due to hypocrisy, as our opponents say, nor yet to some special dose of original virtue, as we are sometimes apt to imagine, but to the circumstances of our history.

Herd Instinct: For Good and Evil

With Germany it is just the reverse. German ambitions are not compatible with the good of mankind. A passage quoted by *The Times* from Erich Kahler puts the matter clearly: "The Germans have arrived too late with their claim for political hegemony. With such a claim they can no longer conquer the world: they can only lay it waste." All Germany seems to have fallen under the dominating influence of Prussia, and of Prussia it has been said with little exaggeration that "the national industry is war." Historically Prussia was a state of soldiers and conquerors, with no secure frontiers, always holding down populations whose conditions have given to the languages of Europe the word "slave." Continual success in war had its effect on the national imagination. A letter is extant from Bismarck to King William, pointing out how each one of the previous kings of Prussia, even the feeblest of them, had added to the territories of the Empire, and his natural duty was to do the same. (The same advice, word for word, that was said over two thousand years ago to have been given to Xerxes by "evil men"! Aeschylus, *Persians*, 753–758). The reaction against Napoleon added fuel to this ardent ambition. The achievement of unity came by means of war, and instead of liberalising Prussia by the influence of southern and western Germany, subjected the whole of Germany to the rule of Prussia. Treitschke fifty years ago, and Reventlow just before 1914, preached the same sort of apocalyptic nationalism which puzzles and revolts us to-day in Hitler or Goebbels. It is what the Greeks called

The Deeper Causes of the War

Hubris, the commonest and most fatal of human faults. It begins by an overweening sense of your own superiority to the rest of mankind; from that it deduces that every action is laudable which helps so superior a being towards his desires. "We have been placed by God in the centre of Europe. We are the heart of our continent. We are the centre of modern history, of the Church, and of Christianity" (Arndt, in 1815). An American exchange professor once told me that, in listening to some ceremonial speeches in the University of Berlin before 1914, he had counted the number of times the word "Deutsch" occurred in a speech of half an hour; it came forty times, rather more than once a minute, and always in a tone of enthusiasm. Perhaps we ought not to be surprised; to quote the late Andrew Bradley, a very sympathetic critic: "After being for long years, even for centuries, a 'Hamlet among the nations'; great, that is to say, in the purely spiritual spheres of religion, philosophy, music, poetry, but, to all appearance, incapable in the world of political action, she found herself on a sudden, five-and-forty years ago, the most powerful state in Europe. She owed this, too, in the main, not to a long and arduous effort of her peoples (for that would have had a different effect), but to a merely military force enlarged and perfected by the unconstitutional action of a statesman and a king. And on the success of this military force and of a Machiavellian diplomacy in creating the Empire there followed (what also was to a large extent new) an immense increase in industrial and commercial activity, in wealth, and in

Herd Instinct: For Good and Evil

population. It would be no great wonder, I think, if any people's head were turned by such a change."

Quite so; by the operation of historical causes, Germany was committed to an intense stimulation of Herd Instinct resulting in ways of thought which were inconsistent with the welfare of Europe or the good of humanity.

These emotions took shape in a philosophical theory, not new indeed; it is explicit in Machiavelli and was probably accepted as obvious in the days of Sargon the First or Og the King of Bashan: but expressed with more meticulous and systematic thoroughness in Germany than in other less philosophical nations. "The State is self-sufficient. Self-regard is its sole duty. The interests of other states are of no account whatever to it, except in so far as they coincide with its own interest. The maintenance of the state justifies every sacrifice, and is superior to every moral rule." Such doctrines can, indeed, be interpreted in a sense that makes them tolerable; for example, it can be held that the interests of all nations, properly understood, do coincide; and that to prevent a total collapse of society the Government of a state is justified in disregarding ordinary moral rules. But German national feeling has not for a moment pretended to interpret them in such a way. It stands boldly up for its own Herd as against Humanity. It openly derides that conception of the brotherhood of man which lies at the basis of modern liberal thought as at the basis of all the great religions. And, we must admit, it inspires a degree

The Deeper Causes of the War

of devotion and self-sacrifice proportionate to its narrowness. The ideal of German *Weltmacht* once accepted, the ambition is quickly transformed into a duty. The noblest race in the world must in mere justice be master of the world. It will inflict suffering on others; that matters little, the inferior races must needs be conquered and subdued. It will go through the fires of suffering itself; they will be purifying fires. Germany is ready for them. In the words of Reventlow twenty-five years ago, Germany must "climb the steps of her Calvary." It becomes to the victim of this delusion a duty, a noble sacrifice, if in pursuit of his divine destiny he devotes himself to the doing and the suffering of extreme evil; for that is what the pursuit of war means.

We English, with our ineradicable wish to believe what is comfortable and good-natured, like to think that the enemy we are fighting is only Hitler, or what we call Hitlerism. But I fear it is only too clear that the Nazi spirit is only an exaggerated and distorted form of a quite old spirit persistent in Germany for at least several generations. As I have written elsewhere:

"The first of many riddles concerning Hitler is the riddle of his rise to power; why was an undistinguished, raucous, verbose, mendacious and half-insane Austrian mystic accepted as the adored leader of a great nation? The answer is clear enough. He represented with paranoiac intensity the prevailing emotion, open and secret, conscious and sub-conscious, of a proud and warlike people, maddened by defeat. When a certain Oxford

Herd Instinct: For Good and Evil

scholar asked Hitler what exactly his policy was, Hitler answered in one passionate word: 'Deutschland!' That was a cry which could wake an echo in every German heart. Treacherous and openly cynical as Hitler might be in other matters, to one cause he was inflexibly true. His whole policy was 'Deutschland,' and naturally Deutschland loved him and accepted the queer mythology with which he explained the inexplicable defeat. It is worth while looking back to his earlier speeches. 'Let us be inhuman! If we rescue Germany we have done the greatest deed in the world. Let us do wrong! If we rescue Germany we have swept away the greatest wrong in the world. Let us be immoral! If our people is rescued we have opened a way for the return of morality' " (*Contemporary Review*, April 20, 1923).

Why do I call the Hitler spirit "distorted" or "depraved," as compared with that of the old Prussian militarists? For three reasons, which can be indicated by the three words, Revenge, Ignorance, Usurpation. The old Prussian was an arrogant conqueror, ready like most conquerors to resort to violence and trickery if they would help him to extend his conquests. In Hitler we have the same spirit, embittered and infuriated by an inexplicable defeat and an insatiable longing for revenge. The old Prussian was an aristocrat, with manners which were overbearing and arrogant but preserved a certain dignity, with methods which were highly unscrupulous but used a certain economy in its breaches of faith. The Nazi movement is **uneducated**: its manners are bad; its

The Deeper Causes of the War

language in diplomacy is utterly unlike that of civilised countries; its breaches of faith are on a scale quite new to Europe, its propaganda seems to be intended for the ears of a very uncritical and unreflecting audience. Thirdly, the old Prussian was the loyal servant of an established hereditary monarchy and devoted to the institutions of his country. When he acted unconstitutionally it was because he considered the claims of his King superior to those of any paper constitution. Hitler is a usurper; like Mussolini and Stalin and most of the dictators now dominating the world, he holds his power not by any long-recognised traditional right, but by the constant assertion and advertisement of personal claims. It is the curse of these usurpers that they can never stay quiet, never retreat or withdraw, never cease to play the Superman. They are only secure when the Herd Instinct of their people is in a state of fever; and consequently it is one of the essential features of the Nazi system that it deliberately keeps the war fever permanent. I often think with sympathy of the principle which Talleyrand successfully asserted at the Congress of Vienna, that the Allies had not been fighting against France, but against Usurpation in support of Legitimacy. Our idea of legitimacy would now be different from that of the Vienna monarchists; but if we interpret the word as meaning the reign of law as against the anarchy of usurpation, I should be quite prepared to accept that as a statement of our cause to-day.

But there is another symptom of the Hitler régime,

Herd Instinct: For Good and Evil

regarded as a stimulation of Herd Instinct, which seems to me clearly pathological. Any healthy Herd Instinct demands active benevolence towards members of the Herd. In Hitler's Germany, the impulse to fight, to beat, crush, torture, humiliate the Herd's enemies has reached such a pitch that it seeks its victims in the Herd itself. The usurper's suppression of dangerous rivals is normal enough. But the Nazis' savage oppression of all outside his own faction, of pacifists, Liberals, Social Democrats, Communists, of Catholics and other Christians who own an allegiance to something beyond the State, and above all, of course, of the Jews, goes far beyond the ordinary limits of political precaution even as practised by usurpers. It is not precaution but revenge; vicarious revenge; revenge on the victims you can get hold of, since the real enemy is out of your power. It is the Herd maddened by passion turning and rending itself.

Where has our argument led us? We see this war, and indeed these long years of crisis, as a conflict between two great human Herds; both with blood-stained histories in the past, since man is by nature a predatory carnivore, but at present differing in their habits, ideals and practical aims. The British Herd, long humanised by the insular security of its capital, engaged in the protection of a vast and increasing multitude of peoples whom it accepts as members and friends; and so widespread in its interests that war in any part of the world constitutes an active danger not merely to its commerce, but to its life.

The Deeper Causes of the War

It seeks no conquests or accessions of territory; its interest demands the general welfare of the world and peace indivisible. The German Herd, closely knit together by successful war, dissatisfied with its great position and determined to obtain by violent methods all and more than all that any other nation now holds; trained to idealise war, and obsessed by ambitions which can only be fulfilled by the wrecking of world order, is forced to inculcate and inflame in its members the destructive elements of the Herd instinct and thus to place its highest value on the power to do the maximum of evil to mankind. For that, in simple terms, is what war is.

There is the conflict; it is between two principles, or two attitudes towards the world. The cult of all normal human values or the cult of war. If Germany wins, war wins. It is easy to turn a nation from the cult of normal values to the cult of war. You have only to beat them until they fight. In a superficial sense Germany has done it to us now, and if the war is prolonged the injury to our whole nature may, in spite of all the efforts of individual good men, become deep and irremediable. That is one of the many evils of war.

If we win, as seems probable, we have a vastly harder task, to turn Germany from the cult of War to the cult of Peace; and not Germany only. Has not this cult of War—this attitude well expressed in Goebbels's phrase: "What matters is not who is right but who wins"—

Herd Instinct: For Good and Evil

spread far beyond the boundaries of Germany? What of Italy, of Japan, of Russia, of the various dictatorships of eastern and south-eastern Europe? Can they ever acquire what is called "the League spirit"? Have they not all increasingly, year by year, moved ever towards the cult of Force and the rejection of Morality? True; they have. But that, we may hope, is merely the natural result of the ever-increasing success of the militarist dictatorships and the repeated humiliations and retreats of the democracies. Besides, it seems that all the others draw their inspiration from Germany. Germany has supplied both the theory and the practical encouragement. If one asks why Japan successfully defied the League, why Italy was able to take Abyssinia in spite of Great Britain and openly to mock us with the farce of Non-intervention in Spain, the answer is always "because the aggressors were backed by Germany and the champions of world order were afraid." If Germany is obviously and conspicuously defeated a second time, we may hope that the smaller nations will see that the forces of law are really the stronger. The gangster in his war against society wins success after success. It looks as if his methods were the real dictates of nature. But society generally wins in the end. A Chinese friend surprised and comforted me the other day. I was expressing regret that, owing to the war with Germany, Britain was unable to give any effective help to the Chinese Republic against the invaders; and he said, "You are doing what is best for us. If you can strike down

The Deeper Causes of the War

Germany, you will have struck the centre of the forces that are our enemies." I think this is on the whole true. If we can defeat Germany the forces of militarism throughout the world will have received a fatal blow. If we can turn Germany towards Peace and Co-operation we shall have saved civilisation. But can we do so?

Can we do much by remedying grievances? I devoutly wish we could, but I doubt it. In 1914 Germany had no grievances. One of our chief difficulties in trying to make friends with her in the years before that time was that we had no differences to settle. Yet it was in 1914, when she had nothing to ask of us, she made her great bid for *Weltmacht*. And similarly now with the exception of the colonies, where other important considerations come in and purely national solutions are impossible, there is no particular grievance resulting from the Peace Treaties which has not been already removed . . . except one, the real, vital and unforgivable wrong to militarist Germany, that she was defeated in the War.

Not much can be done in the way of removing grievances; but any help that can be given towards improving the economic condition of the German people should of course be given generously; and every possible sympathy shown to those forces in Germany that make for peace; every opportunity seized of recognising or creating a close co-operation till the warring herds of Europe can become one herd. Our main business is to convince the German nation, and

Herd Instinct: For Good and Evil

its rulers, not merely that War does not pay but also that Peace does. The first lesson is not in itself difficult. We may hope it will be taught by a second unsuccessful war, as it is already being taught to Japan by an indecisive war, and to Italy by two eminently successful wars. All the war-makers, if my information is correct, are learning their bitter lesson. What is much harder is to destroy the ingrained belief that War is inherently noble, and is the only path by which a self-respecting Germany can attain her true station upon earth, even if it be a path of repeated suffering. To correct that delusion we shall have to combat the intensive education of one generation of Nazis; a long national tradition dating from long before Bismarck and Frederick the Great; and not only that, but also a primeval instinctive tendency in the human race, both male and female, to admire and exalt above all other objects the strong man, the fighter and the conqueror. It needs civilisation, it needs second thoughts, to realise that Napoleon and Caesar and Alexander are not really the highest types of humanity, that War-making is not a glory but a crime.

Can we expect any such conversion in Germany? Other peoples have been converted. There has been a great change in France since Napoleon's failure. A great change in this country since the Boer War. An immense change in those Scandinavian peoples who were once the terror of Europe. We, no doubt, have a liberal and parliamentary tradition to help us. Germany

The Deeper Causes of the War

was never liberal, and has had no training in parliamentary or democratic methods. Yet she has a great social and administrative tradition, a very great intellectual and artistic tradition. Those elements might revive and prove a field for national pride, if once the Nazi Government were recognised as guilty of their country's ruin and the perversion of German youth. The "Hamlet of the nations" might again stand on his abandoned pedestal. We might sit again at the feet of German musicians, scientists and philosophers.

Yet what kind of successor to the Hitler Government can be reasonably expected? Well-informed people say it must be either a military government by the Reichswehr or else a Communist revolution. No other body of opinion has maintained itself in any strength under the Nazi terror; certainly no body of liberal and pacific principles. If so, it is a bad look-out; yet is it necessarily so? The successors to Hitler must necessarily be anti-Hitler; they must be against Hitler's war; they must therefore be, for the time at any rate, in favour of a peace policy. And, though the Communists and the Reichswehr may be the only parties capable of fighting the Nazis with their own weapons of violence, it must be remembered that the most real and fundamental opposition to Nazi violence is to be found in those parties which did not use Nazi weapons and are therefore for the moment powerless, but nevertheless have much latent strength; the religious bodies, especially the Catholics, the intellectuals, the Trade Unions and

Herd Instinct: For Good and Evil

Social Democrats and Liberals, and the remains of the cultivated middle class. I do not think we need despair of finding in Germany after the war a Government ready for peace and fair dealing if only a partially ruined world can help such a Government to some tolerable degree of economic well-being.

Why do I treat a Communist Government as on the whole a danger to Peace? Partly because of its inherent tendency to violence, partly because of its association with the great enigma of Russia. This is no question of class prejudice. Communism as an economic system may be quite as satisfactory as most other systems; but if it involves a bloody class war and can only be kept in being by the ghastly weapon which Lenin called "mass terror," we can be sure, first, that no mere change of social organisation is worth the price, and secondly that any change made by those means will be itself fatally poisoned thereby. Class war I regard as Public Enemy Number Two. There are plenty of other possible enemies before us also; but Number One is still that permanent military ambition which has imposed upon Europe five aggressive wars in the limits of a lifetime. Let us be quite clear. If civilisation is to be saved, we *must* live in peaceful and reasonably friendly relations with the German people: no other future is tolerable or even conceivable: at the same time we must remember that even inside every civilised country social order depends partly on constant supervision by the police.

Let us mistrust all apocalyptic solutions. I have

little patience with those who cannot work with fire and resolution for anything short of the Kingdom of Heaven. We shall have, in all likelihood, not an easier but a harder situation to deal with than after 1918; we shall have a more impoverished world, a more bitterly divided world. On the other hand we shall have as an instrument the lessons of a long and bitter experience. Governments and peoples may perhaps have learnt not merely that War is infinitely evil in itself and the source of innumerable further evils, but that in order to be saved from war, they must at all costs stand together to prevent it.

The League of Nations still exists. I have to attend one of its Committees at Geneva this month. Its ideal was, in my judgment, unquestionably right: that all those nations which wish to be saved from war must form a Society of Nations pledged to accept third-party judgment, and above all pledged to mutual protection. I cannot conceive of a Society whose rules should permit one member to make war upon another and leave all others free to supply weapons to the aggressor. Mutual protection is the hardest, but also the most necessary, of the tasks of the civilised world. If our present civilisation cannot rise to it, then civilisation is doomed. But there is another side to the League's work, a side far easier and more constructively beneficent, which is capable, as the Prime Minister said on November 28th, of vastly greater and bolder development. The cooperation of the League states in labour problems, in

Herd Instinct: For Good and Evil

social and economic matters, in the prevention of disease and the improvement of nutrition, co-operation in the realms of science, art and letters—vast realms to which the poison of the war spirit has not yet spread —co-operation in the suppression of great scourges of mankind, such as Slavery, the Traffic in Noxious Drugs, and in the flesh of women and children. All these activities are of high value in themselves, while the mere fact of working at them teaches people and governments the art of co-operation and mutual tolerance— I hardly dare, in such a world as the present, say some approach to the Brotherhood of Man.

Co-operation should be easy between all who are willing to join in the grim effort towards rebuilding an almost ruined world. Co-operation is possible with men of any colour or country, any political constitution, religion or *Weltanschauung* except one. We cannot co-operate with those whose hope and intention is, at the first opportunity, to cut our throats. For them there is only the police.

People speak much of the demoralisation of the times and the general decay of high ideals. I do not quite agree. I see rather a frightful conflict between an army of ideals and standards of public duty higher than the political world has accepted hitherto and the reactions of a backward mass which dreads and hates such ideals and uses every weapon to resist them. The World War itself, as Professor Pollard said at the time, was a wild protest against the growing unity of Europe. No doubt it has left its harvest of evil. There is more nationalism, more autarky, more suppression of truth, more insistence on war and militarism, and certainly more hideous cruelty than in the nineteenth or eighteenth century; but are these not all reactions against contrary tendencies which have become so widespread and overwhelming that the sinister interests find themselves goaded to madness? Which after all is the main stream, and which the mere rage and splash of a backwash where the rushing water meets an obstacle? Does not the ruling tendency of the time point towards the overpassing of national boundaries, towards international co-operation in countless forms, towards an increased knowledge of foreign countries, increased travel, increased communication? Is not international trade and the whole economic *nexus* between nations so swiftly on the increase that nations, even well-meaning nations, have felt an impulse to protect themselves against it? Has not the spread of news and opinion from country to country by means of telegraph, telephone and radio become irresistibly swift and strong, and so caused the desperate attempts of the stupider nations to prevent it? And as for militarism and cruelty, horrible as these are, can we not at least point to two large items on the other side of the ledger: the vast regions of the world in which, as the Warden of All Souls showed in the first of these lectures, Peace reigns secure and war is condemned by general consent as a wickedness and a folly; and secondly the immense growth in all the

Herd Instinct: For Good and Evil

Western countries of the social conscience, of education, both moral and intellectual, and of humane feeling towards all sentient things? The great movement of human progress, gaining impetus throughout the nineteenth century, and accelerating since then with surprising suddenness, has raised against itself a compact of frightful obstacles; some are natural, some artificial. They are very evil; they seem very strong, but the imponderables are against them. They are not the main stream.

III

SOWING AND REAPING

by

The Rt. Hon. Viscount Samuel
G.C.B., G.B.E., HON.D.C.L.

EVERY event is the effect, not of one, but of many causes. Whether it be the fall of a raindrop or the making of a constitution, the flash of a thought in a human brain, a birth or a death or the outbreak of a war—whatever it may be, every event is the consequence of a vast number of earlier events, inter-acting, combining. We can see a few of the causes at work close at hand; we know that each one of those is the result of a congeries of other more distant causes; and each of them of others again—spreading out and back, farther and farther, till they extend to infinite numbers in illimitable time. It is the task of the thinker, studying some occurrence, to identify the proximate causes; to disentangle them; to trace back, so far as he can, the prior causes; to evaluate; and to draw the moral, and say "if this is something to be repeated, then repeat those events that brought it about; if to be avoided, then avoid them."

This war—everyone sees that it is the consequence of a number of events in the political sphere and in the

Sowing and Reaping

economic. It would be travelling too far to explore through centuries along the paths of history: the German-French rivalry—Louis Quatorze, Frederick the Great, Napoleon, German militarism answering Napoleon, Bismarck, 1870, Kaiser Wilhelm II, 1914; or the German-British rivalry—industrial expansion, colonial expansion, command of the sea, 1914; or the German-Slav rivalry—Austria against Russia, the struggle in the Balkans, and again 1914. Going back no farther than the defeat of Germany and her allies and the Treaty of Versailles, we discern the proximate causes of this war.

On the economic side—Reparations, the occupation of the Ruhr, German inflation and the ruin of the middle classes; the contraction in the imports and exports of the United States, followed by the world-wide depression of 1929; the failure of the World Economic Conference; the unemployment of thirty million workers in the industrial countries, Germany suffering among the worst. On the political side—the reluctance of the Allies to disarm; the failure of the Disarmament Conference; the League of Nations, standing for the Rule of Law, but making no provision for amending the law, appearing merely as guardian of the *status quo*; the League condemning Italian aggression in Abyssinia, adopting Sanctions, but not pressing them home, and impotent thenceforth to control events. Lastly, deep discontent, social and national, in Germany; Communist and Nationalist movements; the rise of the Nazis, and Hitler.

I do no more than enumerate, and only the chief of

The Deeper Causes of the War

the events, so well known, which in combination have given us the situation that we have. If we were a body of economists meeting here to-day, it would be our function to examine the economic causes, and to draw deductions. If we met as politicians, we should consider the political causes. Meeting as students of philosophy, our task is to search behind the economic and political causes, and to find the ideas by which they themselves were set in motion.

For economics and politics are not self-contained sciences, which can be studied in isolation. The nineteenth-century attempt to posit an economic world, governed by its own laws, with its own manners and customs, failed. It rested on the assumption of an "economic man," animated only by material motives. There are no such men, and therefore there can be no such world. We study now Welfare Economics, and not only Wealth Economics. But as soon as we bring in the factor of welfare we find ourselves in the sphere of ethics; and there is no boundary to separate ethics from philosophy in general, and from religion. So also with politics. You cannot draw a line round Political Science and say: This is a matter of forms of government, limits of State action, and the like. At once you find yourself confronted by such questions as Social Justice, International Duty, the legitimacy of War; and again you are in the sphere of ethics, and therefore of philosophy and religion.

When individual men and women decide on a par-

Sowing and Reaping

ticular occasion that This is right, or That is right, or when they decide not to consider rightness at all, they are determining in some degree, large or small, their own futures, and the future of others, and the future of the world. Those moments of decision are the seminal moments. Then the seeds are sown that sprout in actions, good or evil, in harvests of well-being or disaster. If the decisions are right, the result is welfare; if wrong, the result is suffering. I am one of those who hold that beliefs and actions are to be counted right or wrong just for that reason. They are right if they are calculated to promote welfare—using that term in its widest sense to include many elements, spiritual and intellectual as well as material, social as well as personal, prospective as well as immediate; and that beliefs and actions are wrong when they militate against welfare. I belong to the school who hold that the long pursued attempt of philosophy to find an *a priori* criterion of right and wrong has failed; but that that does not mean that no criterion exists. There is a criterion, but it is *a posteriori*, based upon the experience of mankind. From that experience may be deduced various generalisations. We call them the virtues—truthfulness, courage, honesty, loyalty and the rest. Those qualities are virtues, not because they copy a pattern laid up in a Platonic Heaven, but because the practice of them conduces to welfare, in that wide sense. And the vices are vices because the practice of them militates against welfare.

Those who believe that wars make in the long run

The Deeper Causes of the War

for human well-being will believe that war is a good thing in itself, and that there is no reason to think that the decisions that have led to a particular war need have been wrong decisions. But I am speaking to an audience most, or all, of whom will hold that wars, at all events in the present age and between so-called civilised Powers, do not conduce to welfare; that the war in which we are now engaged is not a good thing, to be welcomed, but an evil thing to be deplored; and therefore that the decisions which caused the war were wrong decisions. I start, at all events, from that standpoint.

Let us consider, then, what were the philosophic or religious ideas which were behind the economic and political factors that gave rise to the war. And I do not think it is prejudice that leads us to say that it is the ideas which were current in Germany that are the most relevant. For although the Allied Powers have great responsibility, on account of the imposition of impossible Reparations, and on account of the refusal to fulfil the promise of a general disarmament, neither of those issues was incapable of settlement without war; the Reparations question was in fact settled without war. There is no doubt that Britain and France were most eager throughout for peace to be preserved; they showed it by their acquiescence in the reduction, and then the stoppage of Reparation payments, the re-occupation of the Rhineland, the Anschluss with Austria, and even in the recovery, by open threat of force, of the Sudetenland. We have the right to believe that posterity will judge

Sowing and Reaping

aggressiveness and impatience on the German side to have been the decisive factor. The National-Socialist Government was the embodiment of that spirit, and its agent; and our main task, therefore, is to examine the philosophic and religious ideas which underlie Nazi policy. For there is a definite creed which underlies it. Just as history recognises that the French Revolution was the outcome of the philosophy of Voltaire, Rousseau and the Encyclopédistes, fermenting in the body of the *ancien régime,* so the present war must be recognised to be the outcome, primarily, of the Nazi philosophy fermenting in the body of post-Versailles Germany.

The harm done by the Nazi creed is due to the fact that, while giving right answers to some of the great questions in debate in our present civilisation, it gave wrong answers to a greater number, and those including some of the most vital. (Let me repeat that by Right and Wrong, I mean conducive to welfare, of Germans and of others, or not conducive to welfare.)

The questions to which wrong answers were given may perhaps be summarised thus:—

Has a State duties only to its own people, and none to other peoples?

Is any action legitimate which will promote the immediate interest of the particular State?

Ought War to be maintained as an institution on account of the virtues it evokes, and other benefits it brings?

The Deeper Causes of the War

Are the principles of Race and Soil a right basis for a nation's policy?

Should the control of a country's affairs be entrusted to an individual, and loyalty to him be identified with patriotism?

Does the citizen exist for the sake of the State, and not the State for the sake of the citizen?

Should the State direct all forms of education and information, in order to promote its own ideas, and suppress all other ideas; and this with little regard to truth or falsity?

Is the Christian ethic, in its broad outlines, to be rejected, ruthlessness praised as a virtue, justice and compassion condemned as weakness?

The questions to which most of us might say that right answers had been given are these:—

Does the civilisation of the modern world deny social justice to a large proportion of the populations?

Ought the improvement of industrial conditions, and of environment in general, together with the ultimate disappearance of class distinctions, to be a chief aim of social effort?

An Address of this character allows no scope for examining these propositions one by one. But it will not be disputed in any quarter that the Nazi creed says Yes to all of them. Clearly the result has been good as regards the second section, infinitely harmful as regards the first. In the fact that wrong answers have been given

Sowing and Reaping

to those questions we may discern the deeper causes of the present war.

Let us go one stage farther back and consider why the wrong answers were given.

Not necessarily because of the sinfulness of human nature. Bad decisions may be due to bad character, but also to bad judgment. The so-called Wars of Religion were fought on both sides from the highest motives. The authors of the Inquisition were often men of saintly life. Everyone nowadays claims some sort of moral justification for his acts. The Nazi leaders seek to persuade others, and may have persuaded themselves, that their aims are right; and that their methods, even if questionable in themselves, are justified by the ends they serve. In support they quote a whole literature of history and philosophy.

When Plato said that the human race would never have rest from their evils "until philosophers were kings, or the kings and princes of this world have the spirit and power of philosophy," he assumed that philosophers would be men who not only were "lovers of Wisdom," but would woo her successfully. In this he was rash, for many fail to win her favour. A king who was a bad philosopher might make a far worse king than one who governed by rule of thumb. If you have read a work which has had a wide influence on present German thought, Oswald Spengler's *The Decline of the West*,[1]

[1] London: George Allen & Unwin Ltd.

The Deeper Causes of the War

you will have gone through a thousand pages packed with bad philosophy; and if you have read its predecessor, which may have had even greater influence—Houston Stewart Chamberlain's *The Foundations of the Nineteenth Century*[1]—you will have traversed an equal stretch of distorted history.

Doctrines of Hegel and of Nietzsche have furnished other materials for the Nazi creed. Nietzsche, it is true, said many things in an opposite sense. For example: "To affirm that the State is the highest end of man and that there is no higher duty than to serve it, I regard this not a relapse into paganism but into stupidity"; "Have nothing to do with anyone involved in that brazen humbug of racialism"; "I wage war on anti-Semitism, which dissipates and poisons so much precious energy"; "Grant, oh God, that we may always have a free mind, and all the rest you may keep for yourself." But Nietzsche, for all his trenchant criticism of shams and cants and his fiery exhortations to abandon sloth and rise to heroic action, propounded a system of morals—or non-morals—irrational and perverse, which must bear no small responsibility for the evils of Nazism. In Italy as well as in Germany there have been found intellectuals to preach the full creed of anti-intellectualism. This means in the end that "emotionalism and blind faith are preferred to intellect and knowledge." Europe once accepted that creed—and sank into the Dark Ages.

Bad philosophies take hold for lack of better. I have

[1] London: John Lane.

Sowing and Reaping

heard it said that "Hitler is a vacuum phenomenon." The vacuum exists because neither the philosophy predominant in the schools, nor, it must be said, the religion offered in the churches, satisfy the mental and spiritual needs of the modern world. The facts around us show quite clearly that they are not effective either to direct the minds of the leaders or to control the actions of the masses.

I am expressing a personal view, which will certainly be unacceptable to many of those present, when I submit that, so far as philosophy is concerned, the fault lies in the influence allowed, for more than a century throughout Europe and America, to the teachings of the Idealist school. Berkeley, Kant, Hegel and their many followers, have been allowed to lead human thought, and they have led it into a cul-de-sac. Conceptions such as "The Absolute," "The Categorical Imperative," "Ultimate Values," are a dead-end. Critically examined they prove to be without real significance; they have no relation to the universe in which we find ourselves; but they have blocked the advance of thought. On an occasion such as this it is not possible to argue this proposition. And perhaps that is as well! I merely deposit that bomb and retire to a safe distance.

Perhaps I may meet with a larger measure of agreement—although I do not expect a full measure—when I stress the importance of the lessened influence of religion. This is indeed undeniable; if we compare the present century with the nineteenth and the preceding

The Deeper Causes of the War

centuries it is clear beyond question. And it is plain that this lessening of influence is mainly due, on the one hand, to the establishment by science of many facts that are inconsistent with the ancient and medieval theologies, and on the other hand to the tenacity with which the faiths, Western or Eastern, insist upon maintaining those theologies none the less. So long as there is this discrepancy between the orthodox presentations of religion and the kind of spiritual provender that instructed minds are willing now to accept, so long will that vacuum remain.

Into it have flowed all kinds of strange doctrines: "Blood and Soil," "National Destiny," "Christianity a slave-morality," "Action for action's sake." The only things worth living for, we are told, are struggle, conflict, victory; till at last we come to Mussolini's maxim, stencilled on the walls in town and village throughout Italy—"Credere, Obbedire, Combattere," Believe, Obey, Fight—surely the most degrading rule of life ever offered to a nation. Mixed with this farrago are two other appeals; each of them very strong, their strength more than doubled by their combination—the appeal to the working-classes of material interest and the appeal to every citizen of patriotism.

Formerly Socialism and Nationalism were seldom friends and never allies. The Socialist was usually an internationalist, and the patriot, with militarist tendencies, was usually an anti-Socialist. Now Mussolini, Hitler and Stalin have shown how to combine elements of real

Sowing and Reaping

Socialism with a full-blooded Nationalism. As Mr. Walter Lippmann says, "The fascist appeal combines the emotions of patriotism with the grievances of the proletariat. Those who have been socialists become national socialists. The class war is diverted toward international war."

In a time when there is economic suffering, and in a country where there is a bitter consciousness of national defeat, this mixture is highly explosive. Emotions are raised to flash-point. Rational considerations disappear. People say, "This policy may well prove disastrous, but nothing can be worse than our present conditions. At all events these leaders will do *something*; and anything is better than nothing." So they surrender liberty, accept tyranny, and invite disaster. Hence Hitlerism.

There was a period during the Great Depression when it seemed as though those ideas might sweep over the greater part of the world, including countries not defeated in the war. But it proved not to be so. The English-speaking peoples—less attracted to general theories than the Teuton, or the Latin, or the Slav; less interested in any kind of *Weltanschauung*; more experienced in the practice of self-government—proved immune to National-Socialism, Fascism and Communism. In this country, whenever the issue is tested at parliamentary or local elections, it is clear that not more than two in a hundred of the voters will support either of those policies. In the Dominions and in the United States it is much the same. Furthermore, those everywhere who are religious-

The Deeper Causes of the War

minded, in whatever degree, whether accepting the traditional faiths in their fullness or not, are utterly alienated by doctrines that are of the essence of those political creeds. It is no accident or coincidence—it arises from the very nature of the case—that Nazi-Germany in this war finds herself condemned by every one of the great organised religions—Catholic or Protestant, Jewish or Mahommedan, Buddhist, Hindu or Confucian. There is an exception—the Shintoism of Japan; but Shintoism is less a religion than a nationalism clothed in a mythology.

Thus the war has come, from the clash when the dynamic energy of National-Socialism was withstood by the forces, now united in resistance, of both rationalism and religion. Fascism (which includes the Phalangism of Spain), Communism and Shintoism are in sympathy with many, perhaps most, of the Nazi principles; and not much was wanting for the countries where those doctrines are powerful to have ranked themselves at Germany's side in the battle. They have been deterred, at all events up to the present, partly because of the existence of countervailing forces, especially Catholicism in Italy and Spain; partly by considerations of prudence—the unpromising aspect of the balance of military and economic power.

Let us scan over our genealogy of the war, before turning to the lessons to be drawn for the future.

At the first remove we have the decisions of Hitler on

Sowing and Reaping

Czecho-Slovakia and Poland, applying the policy of National-Socialism. At the second remove we have a number of political and economic events, in Germany and elsewhere, spread over the twenty years from the end of the Great War; events which, in combination, produced the Nazi party, fostered its rise, and permitted its ultimate triumph. Although the errors of the Allies contributed to the result, they need not have led to another war if it had not been for the spirit at large in Germany. At the third remove we find the philosophy of Nazism and Fascism, embodying ideas drawn from various writers on history and philosophy. And at the fourth remove we have the failure of philosophy and religion to furnish any body of right belief or any code of right action, which could command effectively the assent and obedience of the modern world. Thereby room was left for wrong doctrines to take hold on multitudes of minds, astray in a world of material distress and political confusion.

Now as to the future. Let us in the first place discard all ideas of impersonal, undefined "forces" which will determine our fate irrespective of our own decisions and actions. The word "Destiny" appears and reappears all through Spengler's volumes; it is indeed his key-word. How it permeates German thought may be instanced by the fact that Field-Marshal Goering, in the speech of welcome which he addressed to Herr Hitler on his triumphal return to Berlin after the entry into Prague, said, two or three times over, that that event, like the

The Deeper Causes of the War

previous annexations, was the fulfilment of German "destiny"; Hitler was the chosen agent of "destiny." Even in this country the same conception has found expression, though rarely. It was the root of Thomas Hardy's pessimism. In his great epic drama *The Dynasts*, Hardy shows us the Napoleonic armies like columns of ants crawling across Europe; the armies, the statesmen in their Councils, the people in their homes—all of them acting in obedience to an Immanent Will; while the Spirit Ironic, and the Spirit Sinister, and the Spirit of the Pities, look on aloof. The Will itself acts without consciousness:

> Like a knitter drowsed,
> Whose fingers play in skilled unmindfulness,
> The Will has woven with an absent heed
> Since life first was; and ever will so weave.

And this idea of some impersonal "force" was at the base also of the optimistic faith, equally unfounded, which many thinkers of the nineteenth century drew from the discovery of the so-called "law" of evolution. They found there an assurance of a progress that was certain because automatic. But evolution is not a "law," in the sense of a command that will be fulfilled; it is no more than a name for a process. That process has indeed brought about an upward advance; but over aeons of time, and with innumerable retrogressions and failures, as both biology and human history plainly show. Whole species and genera have deteriorated into parasites, or

Sowing and Reaping

become extinct; one after another, civilisations have declined and disappeared; ages of enlightenment have been succeeded, not by greater enlightenment, but by ages of darkness.

Putting aside, then, these conceptions both of destined evil and of destined good, we come back to the true doctrine, that as men sow, individually or collectively, so shall they also reap; and it is for them to decide whether they shall sow wheat or tares. It is experience that tells us on what kind of plant we may be nourished and with what kind we starve.

There is need, I suggest, of a new science—the Science of Human Experience. History, as we teach and learn it, comprises both too much and too little. Too much, because it includes the dramatic, the personal and the literary on an equal footing with the facts that are materials for generalisations of scientific value. We would not willingly lose the artistic element in history; it gives pleasure and it gives inspiration; but it is well to distinguish it from the scientific element. And history has included too little: it has dwelt on political and military events, and on the influence of personalities; but it usually omits, or gives insufficient weight to the physiological side of human development; the influence of environment on man, and man's influence on environment; the economic factors; and the effects of religious and philosophic ideas. In the making of the human story all these take part; and it is from that story as a whole that we may draw guidance. I see then, rising in the

The Deeper Causes of the War

future, a great comprehensive Science of Human Experience. In Arnold Toynbee's outstanding book, *A Study of History*, we may find a pioneer work in that science.

Philosophy, I am profoundly convinced, must base itself more and more upon the teaching of human experience and upon what are termed the Natural Sciences; and less upon logic and metaphysical dialectics concerned merely with speculations. When it does this, philosophy will take again its rightful place, leading the leaders of thought, and, through thought, controlling action. But it must submit to one other condition: to the duty of being definite in meaning and comprehensible in style. I was reading again lately Samuel Butler's *Erewhon Re-visited*, and I came upon this passage, describing a gathering of notabilities:—

> There was Dr. Downie, Professor of Logomachy, and perhaps the most subtle dialectician in Erewhon. He could say Nothing in more words than any man of his generation. His textbook on the *Art of Obscuring Issues* had passed through ten or twelve editions, and was in the hands of all aspirants for academic distinction. He had earned a high reputation for sobriety of judgment by resolutely refusing to have definite views on any subject; so safe a man was he considered, that while still quite young he had been appointed to the lucrative post of Thinker in Ordinary to the Royal Family.

Whether there are any Professor Downies nowadays,

Sowing and Reaping

and nearer home than Erewhon, I should not venture even to inquire.

Side by side with a philosophy linked to science there is need of a religion allied with both. Religion, bringing in the elements of emotion, poetry, tradition, is essential to supplement the rationality of philosophy and to penetrate the vast province that lies outside the scope of science.

Religion is not likely to become uniform; different presentations are needed to meet the differences of history, race, sex and individual temperament. But to many who take an objective view—however much those may differ who see the problems of religion only subjectively—it seems that two things will be found essential always and everywhere. First, that the beliefs that are vital shall be disentangled from legend and myth; that the ancient Theologies, which once were paths to Deity but now are often hindrances, should no longer be allowed to interpose a barrier between man and God, and spoil the essential simplicity of spiritual communion. Secondly, that all the various faiths, Western and Eastern, should recognise that they are striving to serve a common purpose, and should emphasise their points of agreement rather than their differences. Religion, if it is to be truly religious, should surely be a force to unify rather than to divide mankind. In this age there are no more wars betweeen Catholic and Protestant, or between Christianity and Islam; but there is still a sense of separateness rather

The Deeper Causes of the War

than of co-operation; and there are still open conflicts between Hindu and Moslem, Sunni and Shiah.

The antagonisms now embroiling the human race have come down to us from a chaotic past, that has left us a heritage of divisions—races, nations, creeds, languages. If one may coin a word after the current pattern, it should be the task of religion to help to de-babelise mankind.

It is now constantly asked: But how can religion command influence in an age of war and suffering; if there be a God, and if "God is Love," why these wars, and the abominations they bring? The answer may be given that the reticence of God is His greatest boon to man. Were there intervention from moment to moment, or even if there were a revealed code of conduct with plain direction for every eventuality, man's freedom would be gone, and with it his greatest glory. He would become, as has been said, "the mere puppet of a divine Ventriloquist." But the cosmic scheme throws him on his own resources. He has to learn that when he suffers it is through his own mistakes; if he would reap well, he must sow rightly.

To inculcate this vital truth is now the task of philosophy, in close alliance with science and with religion. To draw the deductions, and to apply them in the sphere of practical action, is the task of the politician and the economist. It is for them to find the ways to obviate another war—mutual disarmament, freedom of commerce, some form of polity transcending the nations.

Sowing and Reaping

But unless there is *a wish* to avoid war—and not only in some countries, but in all countries—the efforts of statesmen and economists will prove futile. If there are still to be peoples and governments who act upon the conviction that war is in itself not a bad thing but a good thing; or else that good or bad does not matter; that what only matters is strength, struggle, ruthlessness, leading to victory or downfall—if that faith animates nations, then wars there still will be.

Philosophy, then, has the duty to counter this disastrous doctrine; to make it known that the tragic history of many civilisations has clearly proved, as Arnold Toynbee says, that "militarism is suicidal." There was a sage of ancient Egypt who wrote these words—and they are words in which philosophy may proclaim her mission in this troubled age:—

I will speak that which is great. I will make you hear, I will make you to understand a scheme of life which will be enduring, which will make to flourish that life that is real, and enable you to bring your life to an end in peace.

IV

THE WAR AND THE CRISIS FOR THE SPIRIT OF MAN

by

The Very Rev. W. R. Matthews
K.C.V.O., D.D., D.LIT.
Dean of St. Paul's

I VENTURE to bring before you the subject of the War viewed as a spiritual crisis. If there are any ferocious logicians who refuse to admit that words like "spiritual" have any meaning, I must respectfully decline to enter into that preliminary discussion and address myself to those who think they know in a general way what is meant by spirit.

It is a commonplace to remark that the present war is the culmination of a long crisis in human history. The critical period began, no doubt, long before the war of 1914–18, though it was for the most part little observed in those optimistic days, it has been intensified during the peace and has now reached a dreadful climax. Not every war, even on a large scale, has had this character. Of some it could be said that nothing more than the relations between national states and their spheres of influence seemed to be at stake, but by common consent

The War and the Crisis for the Spirit of Man

we feel, perhaps obscurely but nevertheless profoundly, that vaster and deeper issues are involved in the present struggle. The question whether the British Empire shall survive, which is undoubtedly one of those which depend on the result of the war, is itself only part of a wider and even more momentous question.

From the days of Plato, and earlier, philosophers have reflected on the causes of war. The pressure of population, the need for markets, the search for raw material, religious fanaticism, the ambition of conquerors, the thirst for power and glory, all these are causes of war and in the present conflict most of them may be recognised as playing some part. The demand for *Lebensraum*, though it may indeed be based upon a false calculation of real needs, yet is powerful as a motive. The fanaticism of the creed of "blood and soil" has the force of a religious inspiration. The ambition of the conqueror who identifies himself with his nation is evidently present as a cause. In the minds of many this takes the first place among the causes; they speak of "Hitler's war." It is, I think, important to recognise the large amount of truth in this phrase. The philosophical mind feels at home with abstractions and general ideas, it can deal with concepts and with tendencies, but the personality and its will are less tractable by philosophical method. Yet it is important never to lose sight of the fact that persons and their wills determine the course of events. This war has been launched by the volition of one man about whose sanity legitimate doubts may be

The Deeper Causes of the War

entertained. But for his action the war would not have begun. It seems to me difficult to exaggerate the need of keeping fast hold of this truth, which perhaps the plain man is better able to grasp than the philosopher. It is true that, in one important sense, the war was the work of one man. That is the measure of the chaos into which European civilisation had drifted. But it is more than the symptom of our state, it is a guide to future action. I can think of many desirable war-aims, but the one which seems to me fundamental is to secure that never again shall this power of destructive volition be suffered to be in the hands of any man or a group of men. Though we are cajoled by promises of security and a settled Europe on condition that we hand over the direction to an individual or a committee, though they go under the names of World President or World Cabinet, let us remember Hitler's war.

The purely impersonal conception of history is even more fallacious than the opposite view which treats history as the biography of remarkable men. As I have said, the personal and individual are repugnant to the scientific method, for they introduce the element of the contingent and the unpredictable. Yet history as it is lived, the raw material of the historian, the reality which he interprets and misrepresents, is the biographies of millions of men, most of them unremarkable. It consists of what they experienced, what they hoped and believed, and how they passed on their wisdom and folly to their children. That is the reality; everything else is abstraction

The War and the Crisis for the Spirit of Man

and interpretative hypothesis. When we realise this fact, we can understand why men who have played a great part in historical events have often been sceptical of the reconstructions of historians. They know how complex is the web of human life and personal relations. They tend to agree with Sir Robert Walpole, who refused to have history read to him. "For," he said, "I know that must be false."

Nothing could be more contrary to the obvious facts than the illusion that the influence of powerful personalities on the course of events is negligible and that things would have gone on much the same if they had never existed. Who could believe that, had there been no Napoleon I, the history of Europe would have been practically unaltered? I do not wish to be misunderstood. I institute no comparison between Hitler and Napoleon, whose worst legacy has been the creation of an illusion in more than one disordered mind that it has a Napoleonic destiny. But this at least we may affirm: The occurrence of Hitler gave a decisive turn to events. He was one of those unpredictable factors in history which constantly bring to derision the calculations of the wise. That precise combination of the qualities of demagogue, mystic, cool and unscrupulous politician and ruthless seeker for power, might never have happened. But it did happen, and the man thus constituted met the circumstances in which his personality could grow to monstrous proportions and exercise incalculable influence.

Though I maintain that the personal factor in history

The Deeper Causes of the War

is of great moment and that no estimate of the present state of the world can be realistic which minimises the importance of a few individuals—mostly tyrants—I am, of course, very far from holding that the crisis was made by one or two men. It gave them their occasion and they have modified its course. In all probability they have prevented it from finding a peaceful solution, because the clash of principles has appeared to them an opportunity for personal power, but we should evidently be taking a superficial view if we imagined that the purpose of the war is to restrain the ambition of one or two men and nothing more. It is that, but far more momentous issues are being decided; nothing less than the whole future development of the human race and civilisation. The war is the consequence of tendencies which come out of the past, but at the same time it is creating the future. At the moment we may imagine the spirit of mankind standing at the junction of two paths along one of which it must decide to walk. That surely is why there are so few neutrals in mind, though there never were so many neutrals from fear. Throughout the world men feel that something is being decided which is of vital consequence to them.

Two of the most philosophical writers on Nazi Germany have insisted on the necessity of recognising that the Nazi movement is a revolutionary one and, further, of recognising that it is not revolutionary in the commonplace sense of being a revolt of one economic class or of politically depressed sections of the population. It is a

The War and the Crisis for the Spirit of Man

revolt against the foundation assumptions of civilisation as it has existed in Europe, a demand for a new deal far more drastic than any which ever entered the mind of President Roosevelt, because it is a demand for a new scale of values, a new conception of what constitutes the good life for man. Regarded in this deeper way the contrast between the Nazi and the Bolshevist revolutions, which is obvious enough on the surface, appears to be almost negligible compared with their real affinity. Both are conscious breaks with the past, both repudiate the values which have been the inspiration of the existing civilisation, both contain a new concept of the good for man. Both of them are, in short, spiritual revolutions, and the final proof of this is their ability to inspire in their adherents a religious type of enthusiasm and fanaticism. Anyone who has ever tried to reason with a convinced Nazi or Bolshevik will recognise the type. He is exactly like a Christian fundamentalist—with the important exception that he lacks all charity. We are not wrong then when we denounce the German aggression as a war against civilisation. It is at least the outcome of a movement which is in conscious revolt against what we mean by civilisation. But it may be that what we mean by civilisation is not the only possible meaning. It may even be that a better type than ours claims to hold the field. That at least is what, as I suppose, an intelligent Nazi would assert. He would allege that he was standing for the next step in human development, that the old order was outworn and beyond repair. It must give place to the

The Deeper Causes of the War

new. We are confronted then, it may be suggested, with a conflict of civilisations.

I realise that the word "civilisation" is difficult to define and that no one ought to use the word unless he is prepared to say precisely what he understands by it. I must evade the fulfilment of this condition and state quite boldly that I hold every civilisation to be, in its essence, a distinct phase or movement of the human spirit. No one would question the important influence of geographical position, the state of technical skill and knowledge, the economic conditions, but these are not the essential things. What gives the character to a civilisation, what makes it a part of universal history is the complex of ideas and value-judgments which it expresses. The really important question about any period of history, as Professor Troeltsch remarked, is what values did the man of that period seek to realise? If we look behind the contingent events and the sheer failures and stupidities of individuals, we can ask: "What were they really after? What kind of hope gave them the courage to live? What kind of life would they have regarded as good?" I suppose that this may equally well be said of civilisations and the same questions are relevant to them. That this way of looking at the matter is justified is supported by the fact that all the great civilisations have been connected with a religion, which certainly had much to say on the topics of man's nature and his good.

Mr. Drucker, in his valuable book *The End of Economic*

The War and the Crisis for the Spirit of Man

Man, has expressed what is essentially the same thought when he says that behind every civilisation is a conception of the nature of man. Each one, so to speak, is an answer, on a large scale and in the sphere of practical life, to the Psalmist's question: "What is man?" The character and the destiny of the civilisation depend upon the conception of man's nature and of his true good. Of course, we need not hold that the answer to the question What is man? is consciously and explicitly known and believed by every individual, but only that it is clearly grasped by the leading minds and implicitly accepted by the mass. The examples of China, India, Greece, Medæval Europe occur to the mind as illustrations; of each it might be shown that there was within it a dominant conception of the nature of man.

If then we are right in thinking that the deeper meaning of the war is to be found in a conflict between two civilisations, or between civilisation and barbarism, we are led to ask what different complexes of values are implicit in them, what kind of life do they regard as good, and, finally, what contrasting answers are given to the question, What is man?

When we seek to characterise the system or movement which is opposed to us we are met by several difficulties. Perhaps the most formidable is that it appears itself to be in a process of rapid change. The most obvious instance of this is the sudden alteration in the attitude to Bolshevism. It is indeed astonishing that men who have climbed to power partly by posing as the bulwark against

The Deeper Causes of the War

Bolshevism should now be its allies. This might suggest that behind the Nazi drive there is nothing but the naked will for power and an incoherent opportunism. We must remember, however, that Bolshevism itself has changed and that Stalin is a very different kind of tyrant from Lenin. Obviously, however, the opposition to Bolshevism was not of the essence of the Nazi revolution. Another difficulty is the use of "myth" by the exponents of Nazi philosophy. It is not, I think, clear what, for example, Dr. Rosenberg means by a "myth." Plato and other eminent thinkers have used the myth as a vehicle for the conveying of truth which could be expressed only in symbolical form, the presupposition being that there is a truth of which the myth is a shadow. The theorists of Nazism, I think, do not accept the doctrine of an absolute truth or reality, and I hope I do them no injustice when I confess that to me they seem to use the word "myth" as a polite name for a useful lie. The only man who can use myth and remain honest is the one who believes that there is an absolute truth.

The fundamental element in the Nazi conception of man is precisely that of one who has renounced all absolutes; in this Nazism and Bolshevism are at one. We must not be misled by the fact that Hitler, on occasion, appeals to God. The God to whom he appeals, in so far as he is not a mere figure of rhetoric, is not the Christian God, who is the Creator and Judge of all men and the source of all value and good. He is a mythical representation of the Germanic people or the spirit of the

The War and the Crisis for the Spirit of Man

soil. Those who were fired by enthusiasm for the Nazi gospel were men who had lost faith in the old absolutes—truth and goodness—and were as sheep without a shepherd. Man cannot live without an absolute. If he cannot believe in a true absolute, he will believe in a partial and fictitious one. The man who conceives himself to be in relation with a true absolute cannot be wholly dominated by or absorbed in a temporal society. If he accepts the idea of an absolute good or an absolute moral law or of an absolute truth, he is bound to recognise that the claims of the society upon him have definite limits. He has a life beyond it. The justice of men may conflict with the justice which the moral law enjoins upon him, the truth which he sees may contradict the opinion of the tribe. When once the hold upon the absolute has finally relaxed and the conclusion has been reached, not only with the intellect but with the imagination, that all is relative, men are ready to become slaves. For only the exceptional person can endure a permanent state of absolute relativity, if the phrase may be allowed. The vast majority of us need some relative absolute if that is all we can get. There is nowhere to find it but in the herd, the community or the state. The ideal Nazi and Communist man is the completely collectivised individual.

This brings us to the next vital element in the Nazi conception of man. Christ said: "The Sabbath was made for man and not man for the Sabbath." It is a principle of wide application. The state and the community were

The Deeper Causes of the War

made for man and not man for the state. But this is precisely what the Nazi conception denies. The human being has his value and his destiny wholly within the state. The individual must be wholly subordinate to the life and purposes of the state, or the tribe, or, it may be, of the class. But this does not mean simply that the individual ought to be ready to sacrifice himself for the good of the whole. It means that the state, as representing the mythical will of the nation, must be the final authority. What the totalitarian state claims is the whole man, to be the surrogate for the non-existent absolute. What the state demands is *ipso facto* good. What the state pronounces as doctrine to be believed is *ipso facto* true. I do not say that this condition of hypnotic obedience is the universal character of all inhabitants of totalitarian states; the human being is not so easily enslaved; but it is the ideal towards which the energies of the state are directed, by education, by propaganda and by terror. The idea of man implied in this alleged new civilisation is a wholly abstract one. It has taken that aspect of man in which he appears as a social being and made that his sole character.

It is no accident that the totalitarian state should be opposed to religion, but rather a necessity of its nature. The more clearly that state becomes aware of its own being the more definitely it must regard religion as its chief enemy, for religion stands on the affirmation that there is an absolute beyond all the authorities and loyalties of the temporal order. To religion the state,

The War and the Crisis for the Spirit of Man

the race or the class, when set up as the objects of unlimited devotion, must appear as ridiculous idols.

One of the most sinister developments of the new type of civilisation, as it appears to us, is the emergence of the personal dictator. It is indeed astonishing that in the world, which modern science has transformed, the issues of peace or war should rest in the hands of two men. Still more surprising, perhaps, is it that the sickening adulation which was offered to ancient despots should be heard again. "The Führer is always right" echoes the old cry. "It is the voice of a god and not of a man." It is supposed by many that personal dictatorship is a passing and sporadic phenomenon. I do not believe it. The leadership principle is of the essence of the movement. The state, the race or the class cannot be the objects of religious devotion to the mass of the people. They need a more concrete object. The dynamic person, as presented by assiduous propaganda, embodies for the crowd the values for which the state exists. He is the focus as well as the deciding will.

To us who have been nourished in the tradition of Western civilisation the Nazi theory seems to be clotted nonsense, a bizarre collection of illusions, and so indeed it is, but it would be a mistake to imagine that it had no satisfactions to offer of a spiritual kind. To those who have lost hold on the true absolutes it, or some analogous social myth, has almost irresistible attraction. It promises to deliver the individual from the intolerable pain of self-direction in an unintelligible world, and it gives

The Deeper Causes of the War

him the possibility of losing himself in a larger and, as he believes, more valuable whole.

We assert that we are fighting to defend civilisation; we mean, of course, that we are defending civilisation as we understand it and as we have inherited it. If we ask what concept of man is implicit in this civilisation the answer is not easy, for one of the outstanding defects of our civilisation is that incoherence which furnishes our opponents with their most formidable weapons, and this incoherence is reflected in or, as I would prefer to say, is caused by the diverse concepts of man and his good which prevail among us. There are those who think of man simply in biological terms as the most cunning of animals; others again think of him as the economic man of the law of supply and demand and the class conflict. These conceptions of man no doubt have their truth and usefulness, but it is not from them that the most characteristic and noble elements of our culture are derived. I suggest that the fundamental difference is to be found in the prevailing belief about the relation between the individual and the community and the state. It is our tradition that the state exists for the sake of the persons who compose the community. All the values that have any actual existence in life exist in and for persons. Thus, the conviction is very deeply seated in the minds of our people that the person, every person as such, has a being which is not wholly exhausted by his social relations. This conviction is most clearly expressed in the assertion that the individual person has rights over against the community and the state. This faith has survived the philosophical criticism of the idea of individual rights and also much collectivist theorising; the Englishman, and I suppose the Frenchman too, cannot be argued out of his belief that he has, simply because he is a human person, inalienable rights.

No one could assert that the civilisation which we represent has been built up on the principle of the value of personality without qualification. There are only too many grounds for the accusation that we have been false to the ideal which we knew. It is far from being true that our society always treats persons, in Kant's phrase, as "ends in themselves." But admitting all this, we may still hold that this conception of the person as a value is the motive force of any progress that we make and the source of any spiritual significance which our civilisation possesses. In my opinion, this conception of man is historically due to the Christian religion, and in so far as we are fighting for the kind of society in which the person is respected, we are defending Christian civilisation. The Christian doctrine in its fully developed form recognised that man was a social being and that the state was a divine institution, having as its primary duty the promotion of justice. It was very clear that the Christian citizen had an obligation to the state to obey the magistrates and even, as the Articles of Religion have it, at their command "to bear arms and to serve in the wars." But it was equally clear that the individual is a higher type of being than the state or any earthly com-

The Deeper Causes of the War

munity. They pass away, but he is immortal. Human beings are called one by one, are judged one by one and reach their final good, not in some terrestrial Utopia, but in the vision of God. The Christian, having his roots, as he believes, in the Eternal, cannot be absorbed or intimidated by the community.

It is my opinion that only on the basis of some such conception of the nature of man, one, that is, which passes beyond the empirical to the ontological, can personal freedom be either logically defended or, in the long run, actually preserved, because only on such a basis can the person say to the state or the community, "I am greater than thou." But I do not suggest that it is solely on Christian assumptions that personal freedom can be maintained, though, in fact, the idea of freedom has developed in those nations which have come under the influence of Christianity. The essential thing is that the person should know himself to be in contact with and under the authority of some absolute, which transcends the temporal society. This must be held by any theistic creed and also, in another form, by every philosophy which is in the Platonic tradition. The foundation of freedom is, in the words of a German philosopher, *"dass etwas ubermenchliches im Menschen wirkt."* There is a strange prejudice that the acknowledgment of an absolute truth or absolute good is inimical to intellectual freedom. The contrary is the case. It is the man who believes that there is an absolute truth who will be prepared to admit that more of it may have

The War and the Crisis for the Spirit of Man

been revealed to some persons whom the community regards as rebels or innovators. One who admits that there is an absolute good can easily allow that there may be prophets who have seen more of it than he, while one who clings to an arbitrary and spurious absolute of the "blood and soil" type must suppress the prophets at all costs.

Thus, it seems to me that the description of our conflict as a war on behalf of democracy is a somewhat superficial one. I would speak with respect of democracy, which is probably the best form of political organisation, but whether a democracy is good or not depends on the demos. The problem which vexed Bishop Butler, whether a whole people might go mad, seems to have been answered in the affirmative in our days, for there is a sense in which Hitler can be called a democratic leader. It is easy enough to imagine a democracy which would be, from the point of view of an intelligent minority, an appalling tyranny. Freedom is the name of the thing which is really worth fighting for, freedom of thought, freedom of speech and freedom of the person to develop and express his potentialities.

We may briefly consider the strength of these two versions of what civilisation means, not from the standpoint of their material resources but from that of their inherent spiritual qualities. As I have said, there are elements of power in the totalitarian system and ethos. The dictatorial organisation gives obvious advantages in the rapid and drastic dealing with large problems.

The Deeper Causes of the War

Science compels us to resort to large-scale organisation and planning, which are difficult to carry through in a democratic state. The enthusiasm generated by education and propaganda for the revolution, the race and the Leader, gives, for a time, an exhilarating sense of community in effort and sacrifice. But the totalitarian state has the seeds of death in it. It is bound to impose on the mind dogmatic fetters more effective than any ecclesiastic ever dreamed of. There must supervene a slowing-down of the activity of intellect, first in the creative sphere of literature and art, for the poets must sing always the same tune and the philosophers expound always the same theory. Next will come the researches of pure science, which will be hampered by the purging of its ranks in the interest of political orthodoxy, and, not long afterwards, the technical inventiveness and skill, which apply the results of research, will begin to decline. That this is happening already is plain enough. Not all the boosting of propaganda can conceal the fact that the literature which comes from the totalitarian states is dull and repetitive. The vital books come from the exiles. I am inclined to think that, if the Germany of Hitler does not meet with a violent end, it will expire of boredom.

The chief reason, however, for confidence that the civilisation of our enemies cannot stand and cannot point the way for human progress is that it implies a conception of the nature of man which is not true. Man cannot be absorbed without remainder into a community or state,

The War and the Crisis for the Spirit of Man

even though it be invested with religious awe, for he is a creature who cannot live without absolutes, and he cannot be deceived for ever by spurious substitutes. He is a denizen of two worlds, the temporal and the eternal, or to speak religiously, he comes from the dust and is a child of God.

The disadvantages of our type of society are obvious enough and particularly so in times of acute crisis. We have no taste for imposed discipline; it is indeed contrary to our chosen way of life. The unity and discipline which we have must spring from within the community itself. If that can be achieved in full measure, the strength of such a society will be invincible, because it will be constantly and spontaneously renewed. We have to struggle against an incoherence which is partly, no doubt, the result of our qualities, but which may be dangerous. I have suggested that this incoherence is due to the fact that we have not clearly made up our minds on the question, What is man? All that is best in our civilisation comes, as I believe, from a certain answer to that question which is given, in different terms, by Christianity and by the Platonic tradition in philosophy. Even if I have not carried your assent with me, we shall agree, I hope, that there is no more fundamental problem than the nature of man and his true good, and that on our answer to it depends the kind of civilisation we shall try to create. The crisis for the spirit of man will be solved in the minds of men.

V

THE CRISIS OF CIVILISATION

by

Sir Richard Livingstone

D.LITT., LL.D.

TWENTY-TWO years ago an earlier generation, to which some of us belonged, were determined that the Great War should end war, tried to fix national boundaries on just principles, and invoked the League of Nations as the *deus ex machina* to give the tragedy a happy ending. To-day twenty-two years later we are engaged in another war, involving brutalities which no one would have dreamed possible in 1914, such as the mass bombing of civilians and the sinking of passenger and merchant ships; again we hope that it will end war, and again we are calling on a *deus ex machina* to untie our knots, a deity belonging to the same family as his predecessor, though with rather different features, dress and name—Federal Union.

I sometimes wonder if in the face of this terrible sickness of the world, we are not like doctors who prescribe for a patient before they have diagnosed his disease. I am not arguing against Federal Union or the League of Nations or analogous remedies; but these

The Crisis of Civilisation

only touch the symptoms of the disease. That lies far deeper; deeper than Danzig, the control of the Baltic, the oil and wheat of the Middle East; deeper even than Pan-Germanism or the economic difficulties, legitimate claims, injured pride and fanatical romanticism of a great people. And unless we can lay it bare and treat it, our remedies will be only palliatives, that can do no more than keep the patient in uncertain health for a few years. I am pleading for a fundamental diagnosis. A diagnosis on the purely political side has been made in Professor Carr's *The Twenty Years' Crisis*. But while I do not deny the importance of the political causes of the crisis, of which I shall say nothing, there is much more in it than mere politics. Politics alone do not explain the savagery of the Bolshevik Revolution, or the persecution of the Jews and Liberals in Germany, or the treatment of Czecho-Slovakia and Finland, or the reversion to methods of barbarism in a highly civilised age. The crisis is only partly political. It is a crisis of our whole civilisation, and its diagnosis must include other symptoms than the war. Naturally war fills our eyes at the moment—as if there was nothing wrong with us but its misery and destruction and its threat to our civilisation. But what of that civilisation itself? Is war more depressing than the existence of the *Daily Mirror* or the *News of the World*? than intelligence and energy devoted to football pools and like activities? than the tedious and growing preoccupation with sex in plays, films and novels? Is such a civilisation worth

The Deeper Causes of the War

saving? Consider what idea of our era would be formed, if only those characteristic products, its advertisements, films and cheap newspapers survived: or, if the test of any society is how far its life embodies the spirit of the great trinity of goodness, truth and beauty, ask whether our society comes well out of such a test. If Swift were reborn, has the human race sufficiently improved in two hundred years to cause him to alter his picture of the Yahoos and the Houyhnhnms? It is so disappointing, that like a fool who comes into a great property and and gambles it away, we should waste our immense and ever-growing inheritance on trifles, follies and vices in peace time, and finally risk the bankruptcy of war. And it is so puzzling. For with all its corruptions the modern world has so much vitality and goodness, and in some fields such clarity and determination of purpose. For the last hundred years Science has laboured at her palace of many mansions, like those earlier builders who said "Go to; let us build us a city and a tower whose top may reach unto heaven." And the comment on its work might well be the old one "Behold this people is one and they have all one language; and now nothing will be restrained from them which they have imagined to do." In other fields, too, such as economics and administration, a tide of intelligence and energy has been released which seems as though it might carry humanity to its high water mark. How strangely all this contrasts with our scepticisms and wavering purposes and faint hearts in life as a whole!

The Crisis of Civilisation

We understand how to control everything except ourselves. Yet we might well be on the edge of a great age of the world. But are we? Certainly our condition invites a diagnosis and is not likely to improve, if we administer remedies without one.

There is one great diagnosis of the modern world by a man of genius—the diagnosis of Marx. But his analysis omits more than it includes. It has nothing or little to say about most of the weaknesses of modern civilisation mentioned above. It neither illuminates nor explains most of the great figures or forces of history. Religion, patriotism, democracy, liberty, race; goodness, beauty, truth; the great thinkers, scientists, poets— these are all outside its scope. It answers none of the final questions, such as, what are justice and the great virtues, and why should anyone trouble to pursue them; what is the good life or the end of man? It does not even ask them. Communism may be the right economic and political order, but even if the ideal communist state is achieved, these problems will still wait for a solution. Marx was a great man but also a very limited one (put him beside St. Francis or Socrates, and you can take his measure); his subject also, though great, was very limited. But because it is by a man of genius, and because of its learning and intelligibility and because it deals with a problem, at once world-wide and touching closely every one individual of its millions of inhabitants, his diagnosis has attracted universal attention and distracted it from even more important and

The Deeper Causes of the War

more fundamental problems. If we take Communism as the key to world problems, we expose ourselves to the inevitable disillusion that awaits those who mistake the part for the whole. Economic systems have a curious way of fascinating the human mind and presenting themselves as a solution for all its difficulties. So it was with Free Trade: "Commerce," said Cobden, "is the grand panacea." *Panacea!* To-day Communism has replaced Free Trade. It may or may not be a satisfactory economic system, but no sane person can regard it as a theory of life. Establish your communistic state and all the deeper problems of life remain to be solved. As soon as it is working, you will have to ask, What then? How is life to be lived? what are its values? These questions will press for answer; unless indeed, like the Russians, we are too occupied in clearing up the chaos which follows revolution. Communism may be the right political and economic system for the future, but as a diagnosis of our condition it is superficial.

We shall not understand ourselves and our predicament unless we realise what has happened in the last fifty years. Every civilisation grows up round and with a system of beliefs and values, which are its vital principle, the nerve which feeds and keeps it healthy. If that principle perishes, if that nerve is cut, then the structure of society which depended on it still remains, apparently sound and unimpaired, but the life has gone out of it, its self-renewing power is gone, and it declines first into decay and then into death. Those who have lived

The Crisis of Civilisation

through the last fifty years have witnessed the steady and progressive destruction of the soul of Western civilisation; the soul that began, some 1,500 years ago, to make itself a body which grew with time to such size and strength that nothing seemed able to impair its health. Now it is very sick. And, as with many other illnesses, a disease of the soul is mining the health of the body.

The soul of Europe is partly Greek and partly Christian. The vital force of our civilisation comes from two sources, beyond which no others count seriously, from Palestine and from Greece. We may not believe in Christianity, we may not like it, but whether we deplore it or not, the main source in the spiritual life of Europe is Christianity. The influence of Hellenism, especially in this country, is important; witness such prophets of the Victorian age as Mill, Matthew Arnold, Ruskin; but it touches a small class. The mass of the people drew and still draw the best part of their beliefs and standards in life and conduct from Christianity, however confused and diluted in the channels through which they pass. To attack Christianity was ultimately to attack the spiritual life of Europe; to weaken it was to weaken that life. But this elementary truth never occurred to those idealistic and well-intentioned nineteenth-century Liberals, who cleared the ground for Hitler, Stalin and Mussolini.

I am not denying our debt to the Liberals and to their eighteenth-century predecessors. Who would not be

The Deeper Causes of the War

grateful to those who fought for free thought and free speech and attacked corruption or obscurantism in a dominant Church? If Christianity is false, they were wholly right. If it is true, we may complain that they made no effective distinction between the Church and Christianity: as though a man denounced medicine because there are bad doctors, or Liberalism because the Liberal party does not please him. But whether right or wrong, their success carried with it momentous consequences, which we can see better than they. The chief evils from which we are suffering are due to the worship of power and money, and to the disappearance in certain countries of justice and mercy. Is there any bulwark so strong, any witness so perpetual against these evils, as the religion whose two commandments are, "Thou shalt love the Lord thy God and Him only shalt thou serve"; and "Thou shalt love thy neighbour as thyself"? To destroy the Christian element in the life of Europe is to change it beyond recognition.

The work of destruction begins before the nineteenth century, continued through it and was enormously accelerated in the twentieth; the last forty years have been an age of demolition. Think of the popular writers of this period, its "sophists" as a Greek would have called them, the men who were interested in life and society and human nature and wrote about them, and whose works were read in every educated home—writers like Shaw, Wells, Arnold Bennett, Galsworthy, Lytton Strachey, and somewhat later Aldous Huxley, who in

The Crisis of Civilisation

their generation took the place and filled the role played in the Victorian Age by Mill, Carlyle, Ruskin and Matthew Arnold. The contrast is immense, not least in the fact that the moderns are wholly destructive, if not in intention at least in effect. Most of them perhaps had no wish to be anything else; but even Wells, in spite of his constructive instinct, has in fact constructed nothing. They did their work well, so well indeed, that the younger generation, brought up to see the Victorian Age through their eyes, has a curiously inaccurate idea of it. Its foibles and weaknesses and inconsistencies were ruthlessly exposed; its deep and fruitful beliefs were either misrepresented or ignored; but in any case nothing was substituted for them.

In some sense the process was necessary. Each generation, so long as there is life in the human spirit, must and will criticise its predecessor, in order to live its own life. The ground must be ever anew ploughed over and broken up, to give strength and fertility to the new crop. And the nineteenth century was a time for deep ploughing. The world had to reconcile its life with the new forces of scientific thought, which after transforming our views of the material universe, was bound to turn from nature to human life, and there too deeply to affect traditional views in religion, morals and politics. Much has been gained. We have got rid of the Victorian drawing-room and Victorian prudery and Victorian feudalism. Some ridiculous and some unclean spirits have gone out of us. But with them went better spirits.

The Deeper Causes of the War

When the work was done, what was left? Among educated persons, an important minority firmly holding Christian beliefs, and a majority in various stages of intellectual dissolution, many of them vaguely theistic, most perhaps believing that Christian dogma was untenable but that the teaching of Christ should be accepted, others simply agnostic.

> The kings of modern thought are dumb
> Silent they sit and not content
> And wait to see the future come.

Of all moral (and perhaps of all intellectual) positions, the agnostic's is the weakest. It is a position for fine weather, a house built on the sand; but when the rains descend and the floods come and the winds blow and beat on it, the lack of foundation in the house is revealed. There has been nothing more disappointing in recent times than the failure of the intellectuals as a class to stand up to the dictators. They have denounced, protested, complained, collapsed.

Outside the educated world, thought does not work directly; its influence is through the traditions, habits, conventions, taboos which it creates or destroys. In this world too we find dissolution. The form and order and rule of life which grew up under Christian influences have been so weakened that any strong economic or other force can make a breach in it. No clear rule of life has taken its place. For centuries church-going was the great agent in imposing some unity of outlook,

The Crisis of Civilisation

if not a universal philosophy of life. It was much to hear week by week, even with unheeding ears, the words of the sacred books of the greatest of religions. To-day cinema-going has replaced church-going for the masses of the population. It is no equivalent. And so we get our modern civilisation—a civilisation of means without ends, with an ample body but with a meagre soul, with a rich inheritance but without clear values or a ruling principle; a world of which the characteristic figure is Plato's "democratic man," or Peer Gynt, or the man in the parable from whom the unclean spirit went out, who went through dry places seeking rest and finding none.

All this may seem too pessimistic, too apprehensive. There is so much goodness in England. Yes, but is there a philosophy behind it? "No dogma, no Dean," said Disraeli to Dean Stanley, and it is even truer to say "No metaphysic, no morals"—at least in a world which admits the rights of reason. There is a phrase in Plato which exactly describes our condition, "habit without an intellectual principle." There is nothing bad about habit; all people live chiefly by it and no one can live without it, and the English "habit," the national outlook and tradition, is perhaps our greatest national asset. Yet Plato recurs to the danger of living ἔθει ἄνευ φιλοσοφίας, "by habit without an intellectual principle." His point is that mere habit is very well in settled times, but that it does not stand up to severe stresses; and, as a man who lived in a world almost as

The Deeper Causes of the War

difficult as our own, he had reason to know. Recent events in Europe confirm his belief. In 1930 Germany was a highly educated nation, living in the traditions of European religion, morals and civilisation; in 1940 it is a country where truth, liberty, justice and mercy are forgotten words. In the past these virtues had been created, guaranteed and reinforced by the metaphysic of Christian belief: that had imperceptibly worn away, and the house that seemed so stable proved to be without foundations and, struck by the storm, collapsed. It was a mere ἔθος ἄνευ φιλοσοφίας. What happens, in the experience of all of us, to individuals, happened to a people, and for the same reason. Let us not be too confident of our own immunity from a like fate, incredible and remote as it seems. It is easy in a decent world to behave decently, because most people around are doing the same, but change their conditions, and men change with them. Chameleons cannot be confident of retaining their colour, and in a difficult world something more enduring is needed than a habit of good conduct.

What next? Unless it is wholly decadent, no human society remains permanently in this condition, and our world certainly has too much vitality to be long contented with it. After destruction comes construction. The destroyers have done their work; what new house will the European spirit make for itself? That question has been answered in some European countries already. However much we may dislike Nazism, Communism,

The Crisis of Civilisation

Fascism, they are works of constructive genius—works perhaps of the devil but of the devil in creative mood. Hitler, Mussolini, and, in a much lesser degree, Lenin, are the makers of religions as well as of constitutions and it was the religion which gave driving power for their political and economic revolution, and caused the dry bones to live.

There are differences between the three revolutions. That of Russia was chiefly economic and political, though Bolshevism freed and harnessed the hampered brains and unused idealism of an intelligentsia, and from this took for the moment the semblance of a religion. But it was a religion without a real creed; there is no ultimate philosophy behind it. In the absence of such a philosophy, men tend towards money or sex, nations towards mere power politics: and this perhaps explains the recent developments in Russia which have so disappointed its admirers. But the other two European revolutions were at least as much spiritual as political. In Germany and to a less extent in Italy the leaders built a house for the spiritually houseless, gave hope to hopeless men and inspiration to the uninspired, and made life seem a glorious thing. Here is an extract from a contemporary writer.

The world [seen through Fascism] is not this material world which appears on the surface, in which man is an individual separated from all others and standing by himself, and in which he is governed by a natural law that makes him instinctively live a life of selfish and momentary pleasure.

The Deeper Causes of the War

... This positive conception of life is clearly an ethical conception. It covers the whole of reality, not merely the human activity which controls it. No action can be divorced from moral judgment; there is nothing in the world which can be deprived of the value that belongs to everything in its relation to moral ends. Life, therefore [as conceived by the Fascist], is serious, austere, religious: the whole of it is poised in a world supported by the moral and responsible forces of the spirit.[1]

Omit the bracketed words and it might be the Archbishop of York speaking. In fact the speaker is Mussolini.

We may condemn Lenin and Hitler and Mussolini, but let us do them the justice to admit that they are the only great builders of the post-war age. They divined its greatest need and gave their countries a philosophy or a religion, to replace a philosophy and religion which were dead or dying or forgotten. But it is not the old religion of Europe. In Germany and in Italy it has incorporated elements from it, and for the time in both countries and especially in Italy the old religion and the new live uneasily side by side and even have a bowing acquaintance. In the end one will kill the other. Underneath, the new gospel is very different from the old. It does not belong to the Graeco-Christian tradition which for so many centuries ruled Europe, but is a recrudescence of the barbarism which Christianity and Greece did so much to tame.

[1] Oakeshott, *The Social and Political Doctrines of Contemporary Europe*, pp. 164, 165.

The Crisis of Civilisation

Still I think my main argument holds. Recent events in Europe come from a break-up of its spiritual tradition. They are an attempt to fill the void, and illustrate admirably the truth of that immensely profound sentence in Pascal which explains so much in the history both of individuals and of states: *L'esprit croit naturellement et la volonté aime naturellement; de sorte que, faute de vrais objets, il faut qu'ils s'attachent aux faux.*

But what of ourselves? I have no doubt that the democracies, with all their weaknesses, are in the main and continuing stream of human civilisation and that the autocracies are only powerful back eddies. I also believe that we have in ourselves the forces out of which a new world can be made; but as yet they are fluid, in solution, uncrystallised. Unlike Nazis, Fascists and Communists, our philosophy is unexpressed, our faith a vague and fluctuating emotion. Our weakness is in the failure of democracy to find a creed for its instincts. The failure is intelligible. For if it was hard to create Communism or Fascism, it will be still harder to create *something* which has the depth and enduring power of truth—a permanent flame and not the flash of a day. It will need great intellectual power but also that rarer insight which is moral and spiritual. There is our need and our task. Russia, Germany, Italy have their philosophies. They have done their reconstruction and built their houses. Not many Englishmen have any wish to live in them; but what house shall we inhabit? At present we live in an odd building of which

The Deeper Causes of the War

the best parts are our old Graeco-Christian home, damaged a good deal by recent demolition. If the weather remains good, it may last in its present state for a long time yet; but there is uncertainty about the foundations, and some doubt if it would stand up to a season of storms. Most of those who live in it love it; but it excites affection rather than enthusiasm, unlike the imposing new houses of Adolph, Benito and Joseph, which fascinate and inspire not only many of their inhabitants but also some of our own youth: though they too show signs of subsidence and many doubt their stability. Anyhow our old house cannot be left quite as it is. Something must be done to put it in order, and above all we must decide whether we are going to live in it or somewhere else; we cannot go on for ever living half-in, half-out. The decision and the reconstruction is the great work before us. We need a definite philosophy of life and values and standards by which we can judge and act. At present our philosophy is too like that of Jocasta:

εἰκῇ κράτιστον ζῆν ὅπως δύναιτό τις.[1]

Through what agents might our reconstruction come? It might come as in Russia, Italy and Germany through the State, and in that case it will almost certainly be bad. Still if things get very difficult, if large numbers of the educated class in particular find themselves both without

[1] Sophocles, *Oedipus Tyrannus*, 979. "It is best to live at random as one can."

The Crisis of Civilisation

beliefs and without employment—it is the conjunction of these apparently unrelated things that is crucial—their nerve may fail and they may turn to the state and demand that it save them from themselves. Unfortunately the State has almost no qualification for the task except compulsive power. It can enforce but what shall it enforce? The State can keep order, organise, administer—these functions belong to its nature—but what kind of a life shall it organise. That is a question which it cannot answer. It can provide a body, but not a soul. It has no philosophy of the good life. It must look for a philosophy and it has little aptitude for the search. So when the State takes things in hand, we get something inspired by the personality and past of the dictator of the day—in Germany race and empire, in Italy empire and a self-assumed historic role—and round it a queer medley of ideas that happen to be lying about at the moment, good mixed with bad.

A more hopeful agent of reconstruction would be organised religion. There is after all a presumption that Christianity is true. For starting among unlettered men in an obscure dependency of the Roman Empire, it established itself as the dominating belief of Europe; it has lasted 1,900 years; and no one doubts that if its teaching was universally acted on, the problems of the world would be solved. But apart from this the Churches have an advantage, which no other agency has, except the State, that they can touch *all* classes and types. They are fishers of men in general, and carry the pro-

The Deeper Causes of the War

foundest truths to every variety of human nature and capacity in a form in which each can receive and absorb them. So far as their power extends—and fortunately it still extends far—the Churches are the only bodies in the land which present, subject to the many weaknesses which affect any human institution, a definite and noble philosophy of life. Outside them is a confusion of many voices, some good, others bad. The greatest revival would come through the churches. No other revival could be so effective; perhaps no other will be effective at all. Whether it will start in the Churches, is another question. The children have come to the birth. Is there strength to bring forth?

Are there other agents of reconstruction? If that question had been asked in antiquity, there would have been only one answer—philosophy; and philosophers would have been doing the work. But, if such an answer was given in England, everyone would be surprised and many amused. In this point we are not so well off as the Graeco-Roman world, where the two great philosophies of Stoicism and Epicureanism guided the lives of nearly everyone who troubled to think, and where the Cynic missionaries preached a spiritual gospel to wider circles. They were the salt that kept ancient society healthy for at least 500 years. But no modern philosophy fills even a fraction of their place, and to the ordinary Englishman the very word suggests something quite remote from his life, at the sound of which he instinctively shies away. Why is it?

Partly no doubt because the field held by philosophy

The Crisis of Civilisation

in antiquity was for centuries taken over by the churches. They did the spiritual thinking and teaching for Europe. If we look for a modern Cicero or Seneca or Epictetus or Musonius we shall find him in Wesley or Chalmers or Newman or Gore or Inge. Philosophers retired to the study and the unstudious English left them there.

Nor are the English entirely to blame. The philosophers have not helped them. What does the word philosopher call up in the mind of the ordinary Englishman? A person writing on abstruse subjects in a language unintelligible to the ordinary man, and generally writing badly. Summary judgments are never just; nor is this one. Yet it has a certain element of truth. Philosophy in evolving and operating a technique has too often become purely technical and forgotten its original purposes. It is the tendency of all studies, and grows worse when they become part of an educational curriculum. Then they become more and more formalised and technical, they degenerate into instruments for training the mind or, worse still, into subjects for examination. And so we get a philosophy which has forgotten the meaning of its name and, ceasing to be the love of wisdom,

> Shorn and parcelled strains along
> Through beds of sand and matted rushy isles,
> A stream forgetting the bright speed it had
> In its high mountain cradle. . . .
> A foil'd circuitous wanderer.

In this condition it will not fertilise much country.

The Deeper Causes of the War

Yet there are indications that even in this country philosophy can touch life. There are its traditions in the Scotch Universities, where, as philosophy should, it has combined an exoteric with an esoteric side. In England, Green, Nettleship and others have affected men's conduct as well as their intelligence, and there are modern philosophers who can write about subjects in which ordinary men are interested in a language which ordinary men can understand. Everyone here will think of such writers; and I will only mention the admirable works of your President in the Home University Library and the Penguin Series, and one perhaps less familiar instance of philosophy applied to a practical problem in an intelligible way—Professor Broad's *War Thoughts in Peace-time*. No doubt philosophy can in any case only touch a minority; but that minority is very important; it is not less than the educated public; and not merely do the educated in the last resort govern a country, but their views and attitude permeate insensibly the whole nation.

Apart from organised religion, the most universal force is literature which touches in some form everyone who can read, and, through the films, even the illiterate. It is not its business to provide a systematic philosophy, though poets like Dante, Milton and Wordsworth have done something of the sort. Its task is illumination, and by the quality of its light and by the objects it illuminates, it does in fact provide a view of the world. But though its output and level of competence have

The Crisis of Civilisation

been higher than ever before, postwar literature has done nothing to help us. It has been the work of good craftsmen but mediocre human beings. Much of its talent has gone into technique, and much of its creation been in the field of lesser things. There have been some positive voices, but the ablest and clearest have uttered a philosophy not of life but of doubt, decay and death. Much of post-war literature—especially poetry—so far as it dealt with greater issues, has been an angry and ignoble whine. No doubt there is plenty to cry about; so there has been in all ages. But the right response to the evils of the world and even to an evil world is not to complain of the evil but to create good; to write not in the mood of *The Waste Land* or *Point Counterpoint* or *The Forsyte Saga* but in the mood of the *Divina Commedia*, or the *Oedipus Tyrannus*, or *King Lear*, or the *Prometheus Unbound* or the *Prelude* or of such substitutes for these as lesser genius can compass. We have wanted, and not had, the mood of Shelley, a tortured spirit himself and living in a tortured world:

> To suffer woes which Hope thinks infinite;
> To forgive wrongs darker than death or night;
> To defy Power which seems omnipotent;
> To love and bear; to hope till Hope creates
> From its own wreck the thing it contemplates.

But this creative spirit we have not had. At the moment when we needed such creation, there has been no one to create. To-day there are perhaps signs of a change.

The Deeper Causes of the War

I have spoken of the need of a clear philosophy of life, and may seem to have evaded suggesting one—very properly, as I am not a philosopher. But I happened to read Plato for a special purpose last September, and he seemed curiously apposite to the moment. There was the portrait of a dictator, the tyrannical man of the *Republic*, who begins by promising everyone to get them out of their economic difficulties, who constantly stirs up war in order that the people may feel the need of a leader, and uses the war to get rid of his enemies, who quietly puts out of the way any of his supporters that are bold enough to criticise him and has a "purge" of the richer and the better citizens; whose ever-growing army is supported by confiscations of private and sacred property; whose government becomes an open and avowed tyranny and whose country "finds that it has exchanged a limitless and unseasonable liberty for the harshest and bitterest of all slaveries." There too is the dictator's philosophy: that justice is a mere fiction invented by the weak to protect themselves against the strong; but that when a man of sufficient strength and determination appears, he ignores it, tramples laws and conventions under foot and makes himself lord of the world. There too is the answer to the dictator's philosophy; that to ignore justice leads to a chaos in which everyone fights for his own hand and no one prospers, that order is a fundamental principle of political life, and that even if successful, injustice brings unhappiness, because "goodness is the health,

The Crisis of Civilisation

beauty and well-being of the soul, and evil is its disease, deformity, and ill-being." There too is the right attitude to the ultimate problems of life: "A man should persevere till he has achieved one of two things; either he should discover the truth about them for himself or learn it from someone else: or if this is impossible he should take the best and most irrefragable of human theories and make it the raft on which he sails through life."[1] There is the conviction that goodness, beauty, truth and the great virtues are alone permanent and of permanent value; and that "a man may be confident if he casts away the pleasures and ornaments of the body as alien things, and dresses the soul in her own proper jewels, right-mindedness and justice and courage and nobility and truth and so waits the hour of his journey to another world."[2] Such a philosophy may be regarded as complete in itself or as a *praeparatio evangelica* which leads to Christianity. Something like it underlies all that is best in our civilisation, and, if firmly held and followed, would both purify and save it.

[1] *Phaedo*, 85.   [2] Ibid., 114.

VI

SCIENCE AND HUMANE VALUES

by

Sir Richard Gregory, Bart.

F.R.S.

SCIENCE is not often associated with humane values in the public mind. It is usually regarded as a dehumanising influence, to be held responsible for the conversion of beautiful countrysides into grimy industrial scenes, or with clouds of poison gas and high explosive shells—all destructive of natural life and beauty. Such evil uses are perversions of the gifts which modern science has showered upon the human race. The purpose of scientific study is to discover the truth about all things, including man, his instincts and impulses, and his control of them, as well as of the forces of Nature. The true scientific spirit is that of the great French philosopher, Descartes, who said that he studied science "in order to learn how to distinguish truth from falsehood, so as to be clear about my actions and to walk surefootedly in this life."

Three centuries ago, Galileo and other pioneers of experimental science established the right of a man to think for himself in the realm of natural knowledge, and to be free to test all things by direct observation and

Science and Humane Values

experiment, independently of authority or traditional belief. It was in this spirit that the Royal Society of London, founded in 1660 for the promotion of natural knowledge as against supernatural revelation, took for its motto *Nullius in verba*, signifying "not bound by the words of any man." The independence of thought and action now possessed by democratic communities is a direct social consequence of this principle of scientific inquiry. No State or administrative action should be tolerated which would restrain the conditions of intellectual development thus secured.

Freedom of thought and speech, belief and investigation, subject only to the recognition of the same liberty on the part of others, is threatened by the new tyrannies which, through their aggressive militarism and economic nationalism run mad, seek to reduce the citizen to a soulless unit and a condition of moral and intellectual servitude. The existence of economic antagonism and military rivalries among nations is as grave a danger to scientific thought and investigation, upon which so many modern achievements are based, as it is to the continuance of our material civilisation. Science, therefore, must stand for high human values, as against slavery of the spirit of man, if it is to play a fitting part in saving civilisation from the dangers which now threaten it.

In its unswerving loyalty to truth as revealed by independent inquiry and impartial judgment, science promotes one of the noblest human values. Though ethical standards vary in different communities at different stages

The Deeper Causes of the War

of development, certain virtues, possessed in greater or less degree by all human beings, are held in such high esteem as to be regarded as divine. These humane qualities are mercy, goodness and love, knowledge and wisdom, faithfulness and truth, justice and righteousness, compassion, pity and long-suffering. It is by aspiring towards these ideals that the human race differs from other living organisms; and every system of thought or subject of study which includes them in its teaching is promoting the ethical or spiritual evolution of mankind. In the spirit of its pursuit, science can claim association with most of these high attributes, and, in its essential aims, co-operation with all of them.

All ethical systems and religions of the highest type embody these humane principles, the recognition of which represent stages of civilised life. In the study of man and his activities three types of creative development may be recognised; and they are all measured by different standards. In the fine arts the imaginative qualities of the mind appeal primarily to the emotions through stimulation of the aesthetic judgment; material culture is the province of mechanical arts; and science—the domain of reason—is systematic and formulated knowledge in all fields of human understanding—natural, moral, social and political. Natural science, or natural philosophy, is only one division of science as thus defined. The history of civilisation from this point of view is a history of intellectual development in which science has been the chief factor in changing habits of

Science and Humane Values

thought from superficial observation and speculative and anthropomorphic theories of causation to clear concepts, rational conclusions, and progressive principles in the advancement of man and society.

In the most primitive times man had to acquire knowledge of the world of Nature around him in order to survive. The effort to secure the food and shelter necessary for his existence demanded a never-ceasing exploitation of the resources of his environment for the progressive improvement of his material equipment—an equipment which he learned to turn against his fellow-man, no less than against the animal world upon which he preyed for food and clothing, or against which he must defend himself. But in this struggle, even more than on his personal prowess, his skill, and his knowledge of the habits of food plant and animal, man relied upon his imagined understanding of, and his supposed power to control, the hidden causes of the nature and behaviour of the beings and objects of his world; in other words, his will to survive was rooted in magic. Though the magical beliefs of primitive man may seem to us vain and crude, they should not be despised; for in these blind gropings to probe causation in Nature may be seen the remote and humble beginnings of the urge to the understanding of the universe, which is science.

Magic, religion and science are now regarded by most authorities as stages in the development of man's conceptions of his relationship to Nature. Sir James Frazer, in his monumental work, *The Golden Bough,* has shown that the movement of human thought has, on the whole, been from magic, through religion, to science. In magic, man believes that he can, by certain actions of his own, manipulate the established order of Nature to meet his immediate needs. When he finds that he cannot exercise this control, he ceases to rely on his own unaided efforts and ascribes to certain great invisible beings behind the veil of Nature the far-reaching powers which he once thought he possessed himself. Thus magic is gradually superseded by religion, and natural phenomena are believed to be regulated by deities who are like men in kind and are swayed by human passions, but are endowed with powers vastly superior to his. At a much later stage he finds that these gods are only the products of his own imagination, and that they are not servants of his will either to produce good or to avert evil. Then comes the recognition that the laws to which he has to submit or control are those of Nature, and that the study of them constitutes science.

Science here signifies organised knowledge derived from experience; and though in this sense it represents a new attitude of mind towards the universe of Nature, it has to become a social ideal and an emotional force before it can form what is commonly understood by religion. It is only when society recognises that the pursuit of truth by the sage is as divine a purpose as contemplation of it by the saint that the two meet on the sacred ground of religion. Religion is a complex of both thought and emotion, beginning with perception of the vague, the

Science and Humane Values

indefinite and the mysterious, which becomes deeper with increasing knowledge and merges into philosophic speculations on the infinite. As a social force, religious faith constitutes a principle by which to live, whatever its origin or course of evolution.

In early stages of thought, man endowed all animate, and even inanimate, things with the characteristics of life which he himself possessed, and projected his own attributes upon the heavens. As the sun, moon and the five planets then known were deities thus personified, and therefore were objects of worship, it was natural that their appearance and positions should be carefully observed in order to determine the times of religious festivals. Each god or goddess was endowed with special qualities and was regarded as having particular influence upon the earth and mankind; and the supreme god possessed the attributes of many of the others.

There were therefore, in those days, very good reasons for believing that aspects of the heavens, as represented by planetary or other gods appearing in them, directly affected people and events upon the earth. Such associations of celestial bodies with terrestrial affairs form part of many early religious beliefs. When, however, the planets and other heavenly bodies were divested of their gods, and became substance instead of spirit, the essential principle of astrological relationships disappeared.

Astrology implies the existence of separate deities associated with, and controlling the motions of prominent astronomical objects. To believe in it is to

The Deeper Causes of the War

enshrine divine attributes in bodies which are now known to be purely material, and the movements of which are determined by known natural laws. It is only by disregarding such knowledge, and reverting to the pagan religious beliefs of ancient Babylonia, Greece and Rome, that the teaching and guidance of astrology can be accepted by civilised people to-day. That astrological conceptions associated with religious beliefs of five thousand years ago should be exploited by a modern priesthood is a pathetic reminder of the persistence of human credulity, and the slow rate of transition from primitive conceptions to enlightened knowledge.

It is common in these days to think of progress in terms of material development and to leave out of consideration the contacts of science with what is known as "polite" learning—literature, religion and other expressions of the human spirit. The noblest works of man are not, however, represented by great industrial advances, but by the search for the truths upon which they are based, and by the influence of this effort upon personal and social ethics. These intellectual or spiritual associations of science were more common in former times than now, when we are passing through, or perhaps, as it may be, just emerging from, a materialistic age in which they tend generally to be neglected.

Art and literature are usually confined to the expression of what are understood to be the eternal verities of life; and, though their technique and methods change, supreme standards of excellence may be reached at any

Science and Humane Values

epoch. In the fourth and fifth centuries before the Christian era, the works produced by the artistic, philosophic, and literary genius of the Greeks are masterpieces which will command admiration for all time; and ancient Rome, as well as India and China, has each had its golden age of artistic and literary culture. In Western Europe architecture, painting and poetry have similarly reached summit levels of excellence at various epochs and then declined. Progress in any of these arts of expression can only be in the richness of creative ideas, and this is essentially an individual possession. Artists may aspire to emulate the paintings of Raphael or Leonardo da Vinci, but they cannot use the works themselves as canvases upon which to add their own conceptions.

Science, however, differs from the fine arts in the fact that every discovery extends the boundaries of knowledge and may be the starting-point of further progress. It was upon the foundations laid by Kepler and Galileo that Newton was able to construct the universal law of gravitation; and it is by the succession of such discoveries that science advances, while the picture it presents is continually being enlarged and amplified in detail. The time may come when art and literature will be moved by such achievements of the human mind to make manifest their real meaning, and the imagination will be so quickened by the spirit of man reaching out to the stars that artistic and literary response to the beauty and mystery of Nature will be deeper and nobler than ever before.

The Deeper Causes of the War

Freedom to follow the inborn light, and to express the truth revealed by it, is an essential condition of progressive development of human thought and action. At all times there have been reactionary influences against new knowledge of any kind, or the emancipation of the human mind. The advanced views of the Greek philosophers in the latter half of the fifth century before the Christian era did not meet with general acceptance even in that enlightened period. Because Anaxagoras taught that the sun was a mass of flaming matter, he had to leave Athens to save himself from death; and Protagoras, the first of the Sophists, died when fleeing from Athens after he had been convicted of blasphemy. There was, however, no organised repression of liberty of thought; and personal or political reasons were the causes of condemnation for impiety or disturbing teaching to the people. It was because Socrates would not cease to "corrupt the young" and invite public discussion of his philosophy of life that he was condemned to die. Rather than be untrue to his convictions, he accepted death; and he justified his position in words vibrant with exalted principles:

If you propose to acquit me on condition that I abandon my search for truth, I will say: I thank you, O Athenians, but I will obey God, Who, as I believe, set me this task, rather than you, and so long as I have breath and strength I will never cease my occupation with philosophy. I will continue the practice of accosting whomsoever I meet and saying to him, "Are you not ashamed of setting your heart on wealth

Science and Humane Values

and honours while you have no care for wisdom and truth and making your soul better?" I know not what death is—it may be a good thing and I am not afraid of it. But I do know that it is a bad thing to desert one's post and I prefer what may be good to what I know to be bad.

If the biological principles of variation of character, struggle for existence and survival of the fittest are applied to social evolution, then, at any stage of civilisation, good conduct is that which conforms to what is conceived to be high social ideas, and evil is that which is in conflict with them. There are, however, no absolute ethical standards. Good acts are distinguished by their adjustment to the social order, and bad by their failure to do so. Good conduct falls within the order: bad conduct fails to adjust itself and is condemned. Conduct is determined by character, and character in man implies action guided by a will conscious of moral or ethical standards. It may thus be distinguished from the impulse which, in other creatures, represents instinctive reaction to a stimulus.

In what is conceived to be the highest type of civilisation to-day, certain ethical and humane sentiments, such as those of justice, and mercy, and sympathy with the weak and suffering, are possessed and practised by a greater number of the community than ever before. Ancient Greece and Rome represented periods of great intellectual splendour, but, until the time of the Stoics, the sense of justice and humanity did not extend beyond a fellow-citizen. In the rude struggles of the two thousand years terminating in the sixteenth century, little was done to create or foster altruistic attributes of human nature. Yet during the ages when might was right, when violence, cruelty and rapine held sway over Europe, the true, the humane and the just steadily increased and the standards of conduct towards others became ethically higher, until now no people or nation which reverts to such methods can claim to be in the van of modern civilisation.

Whatever convictions may be held as to the future of man or humanity, the standard of goodness is decided by the community. The man who lives a moral life merely because he wishes to save his own soul is not taking a high standard of spiritual action, for his motive is personal profit. He may believe he will be saved from punishment hereafter by being negative to evil, but his life will be of no benefit to the human race unless he is positively good. What existence awaits us when we cross the dark river we cannot say, but stimulus and high endeavour may be found in the hope that each thread of life can assist to form an harmonious pattern, even if the design is not known. Though science may not be able to contribute much to the ultimate problems of spiritual beliefs, it does teach that every action carries with it a consequence—not in another world but this—to be felt either by ourselves or others in our own lifetime or the generations to come.

We have passed the stage when, in order to afford support for Christian belief in general, and the Mosaic account of creation in particular, it was only necessary

Science and Humane Values

to find naturalistic or rationalistic explanations of miraculous and other elements in Biblical records. Such attempts to fit all new knowledge into a system of thought having no claims to scientific accuracy or intention served no useful purpose to the Bible or to science, and to-day would satisfy neither historical students nor naturalists. A much sounder basis can be found by applying evolutionary principles to religious thought, and by studying sacred books as stages in the story of man's progressive discovery in theology. It is only by disregarding history that the idea of a fixed and final theology becomes possible. In science, there are no final interpretations or unchangeable hypotheses; and if the same principle were recognised in theology, religion would share some of the vitality of the natural sciences. Evolution can be regarded by the theologian as merely the means of creation; and the conception of gradual development is not incompatible with Christian theology. It is through the acceptance of the idea of evolution in the spirit as well as in the body of man that the partition which formerly separated religion and science is being dissolved.

The recognition that knowledge of the physical universe is only the bud of a flower which can never be seen in its perfection is the salvation of science. Nature acknowledges no exclusive claims to truth or right of dictatorship in her name, either to this generation or the next. The scientific man has to work for Truth so far as her ways can be comprehended by him, but he is never more than a trustee for posterity, and has no

The Deeper Causes of the War

authority to define the functions or limit the freedom of those who follow him. When men believe that complete truth has been revealed to them, they restrain inquiry and persecute those who fail to see the same light. This position can never be taken in science, which invites investigation, welcomes criticism and rejoices at new truths to supersede or supplement the old.

Just as Copernicus deposed the earth from the position it was supposed to occupy in the universe, so, three centuries later, Darwin placed man in a new relationship to the rest of living creatures. It is often supposed that Darwinism leaves ethical and moral ideas out of consideration and stands only for the doctrine of "Nature, red in tooth and claw"; but this is due to lack of understanding of the principle. Evolution embodies the idea of social ethics and makes the welfare of the community the essential purpose of the life of the creature. The view that Darwinism signifies nothing more than striving after personal or national mastery at all costs is a crude misconception of this great principle, and was repudiated alike by its founder and by Huxley, its most powerful exponent, as contrary to the best ends of civilisation. Nearly fifty years ago, in his inspiring essay on *Evolution and Ethics*, this champion of scientific thought and intellectual liberty expressed the higher meaning of evolution when he said:

The practice of that which is ethically best—what we call goodness or virtue—involves a course of conduct which, in

Science and Humane Values

all respects, is opposed to that which leads to success in the cosmic struggle for existence. In place of ruthless self-assertion it demands self-restraint; in place of thrusting aside, or treading down, all competition, it requires that the individual shall not merely respect but shall help his fellows; its influence is directed, not so much to the survival of the fittest, as to the fitting of as many as possible to survive.

This is the religious message of science; and all the evils of civilised life arise from the neglect of it by individuals and communities.

Many similar declarations from leading scientific authorities in more recent years show that they are keenly conscious of the interrelation between natural science and social problems, and desire to assist in the use of knowledge for the advancement of the human race instead of its degradation. The wise application of science especially involves questions of ethical or humane values, and is linked up closely with the general conditions and standards of the society in which scientific work is carried on; for belief in honesty of purpose, liberty of thought and high ideals of service are essential for creative endeavour in any field of intellectual activity.

Charles Darwin made a notable contribution to this part of ethics when he traced the development of moral principles in human life from the point of view of natural selection in three chapters of his *Descent of Man*. He showed that the higher rules of human conduct are founded upon the social instincts and relate to the welfare of others, while different rules arise from public opinion matured by experience and cultivation. "As man advances in civilisation," he said, "and small tribes are united into larger communities, the simplest reason would tell each individual that he ought to extend his social instincts and sympathies to all the members of the same nation, though personally unknown to him. This point being once reached, there is only an artificial barrier to prevent his sympathies extending to the men of all nations and races."

The evolution of European civilisation may be considered as a series of epochs in which is manifested the play of centripetal and centrifugal forces, making for the integration and disintegration of social unities, and operative in ever increasingly extended fields of human associations—"from tribe to empire." The integrating force, by the expansion of the sphere in which individuals co-operate for the attainment of common ends, makes for the ultimate recognition of the common purpose of mankind as a whole. This force became united in the great kingdoms and empires of the early eastern peoples of different racial and cultural origin and tradition, but who, nevertheless, came to regard themselves as more or less akin, or at least united. On the other hand, the disintegrating force makes for exaggerated nationalism and separatism, such as existed in the Greek city-States.

European history is a struggle between East and West, the results of tribal migrations from Asia into Europe and their resurgence, when the extreme west is reached.

Science and Humane Values

This movement began so far back as late Palaeolithic times possibly, certainly in Neolithic. The migratory struggle in Europe reached its peak of highest intensity in the early centuries of the Christian era; but it is still going on.

Combined with the struggle of West against East is the attempt to integrate the whole or part of Europe. This is only one phase of a movement towards integration which goes back to the earliest stages of man's social history, as in Egypt and Mesopotamia. Napoleon and the League of Nations are examples on a grand scale; but in greater or less degree this movement runs throughout European history; for example, the various Protestant leagues, the Roman empire and the Roman church. Most of these movements have been based on force, but the Pan-Germanic, Pan-Teutonic, Pan-Slavic and Pan-Turanian movements are examples in which race has been urged as the basis of union. This also was the sentimental side of the British empire.

As against these movements towards integration, there have been the centrifugal forces, mostly nationalistic. The centrifugal force in the British empire was responsible for the passing of the Statute of Westminster, which brought the empire to an end, and gave rise to the looser organisation of the British Commonwealth of Nations. The importance of this conception of centripetal and centrifugal forces at work in the development of civilisation is that it represents an effort towards the recognition of a universal brotherhood of man growing out of a

The Deeper Causes of the War

normal development in the evolution of social organization and its frustration.

Though, in the past, war has played a part in the formation of certain peoples, it represents only one phase in the development of civilisation and is a part of a larger whole. Civilisation, it is true, develops through individual peoples, as historically speaking, mankind has been organised on that basis, but we, as heirs of the ages, to use a trite but expressive phrase in this connection, are not interested in the survival of these peoples, except in so far as they have contributed to the general advancement of mankind. The contribution to the advancement by these peoples has not been through their warlike qualities, but by their contributions to humanistic values. The trend of cultural achievement in the advancement of mankind has been to operate through larger and larger unities—tribe, people, nation, confederacy, eliminating war and the struggle for existence as a physical fact and relying more and more on the struggle for existence as between ideas. In other words, in our modern civilisation, ideally speaking, it is no longer the force of arms which binds these unities together—for example, the British Commonwealth of Nations—but the strength of an idea or principle.

At present the idea of democracy is struggling against that of autocracy or totalitarianism. Unfortunately, totalitarianism is wedded to the reactionary idea of nationality, which checks the advance towards the larger communities in which mankind will be united and in

Science and Humane Values

which war will be eliminated. In so far as the idea of war as a "pruning-hook" lends support to national theory, it is reactionary and irrelevant to the true ideal of human progress. It is wrong, because it ignores or misinterprets certain very essential facts, of which the chief is that, beyond a certain phase, the struggle for existence ceases to be a physical struggle and becomes a conflict of ideas; that is, survival is cultural. By this comes about the growth of civilisation. In this growth war is a catastrophe, comparable to a great earthquake or other convulsion of Nature but only incidental to the development which is continually going on in all forms of life.

Even if it be conceded that the fighting instinct of man has promoted the strength of his body and disciplined his mind, or that it encourages the supreme self-sacrifice in support of high ideals, the destruction of life in anger must degrade rather than promote humane values. The spiritual evolution of man, as represented by all that is best in civilisation throughout the ages, and as inspired by the most exalted religious and ethical teachers, has not proceeded in its upward course through war but in spite of it; and it is in the belief in its further development that hope may be found for the future.

The association of science with war, and the prostitution of scientific effort to war purposes, cannot be condemned too strongly, yet few scientific workers would wish to avoid participating in adequate and effective methods of national defence, or to fail in their service to the high humanistic ideals for which science stands.

The Deeper Causes of the War

Every nation has the right to decide upon its own form of government—democratic or autocratic—just as it must be left free to follow its own religious ideals. Each country has its own standards of ethical and social values and cannot easily recognise any other. When, however, the deliberate policy of a State is to impose its system by force upon people who wish to be free and have entirely different ideals, all believers in liberty of conscience and in the principles of natural cultural development should range themselves against such aggression. Judged by its policy and actions, the ideals of Nazi Socialism—apart altogether from the political aims—represent a reversion to degrading primitive instincts; and if ever they should prevail, the best characteristics of modern civilisation would be destroyed.

The essential aims of the Allies in the present war are to defend what are the highest humane values of civilisation—justice, truth, consideration for others and peaceful co-operation—against the doctrine of force and a reversion to the law of the jungle, to which Nazi Germany would subject the world. When right prevails, as history shows it has always done in the end, it is to be hoped that the world will be reconstructed in an international spirit of equity rather than in that of narrow nationalism, aggressive imperialism or racial distinctions, which have been the cause of most conflicts.

Modern war makes no distinction between the destruction of masterpieces of architecture and ammunition dumps; and barbarous aerial bombing of any centre of

Science and Humane Values

life or of beauty seems to be accepted as a means of offensive action by nations which claim to be civilised. Instead of science having to save modern civilisations from being overwhelmed by barbarous hordes, it seems to have provided the means of self-destruction. Man has advanced so little in ethical evolution that he is just as much a barbarian in his use of aerial bombs and poison gas as he was when his weapons were only clubs and arrows.

Such prostitution of the rich gifts with which modern science has endowed the human race must be condemned by all who see, in the general feelings of civilised people to-day, incipient stages in the development of characteristics which distinguish man from other living creatures. The law of the jungle is that of the battle to the strong and the race to the swift. It recognises no right to live except by might; destroys the weak; has no sympathy with suffering and no sense of the humane values. In the struggle for existence man has survived because his physical structure and intelligence have enabled him, individually and in communities, to master the things which would destroy him. His social instincts have at the same time been extended from the family to the tribe, the nation and the empire, and will reach their highest and best when they embrace the world.

The virtues which should be prized most to-day, if civilisation is to mean the evolution of social ethics to a noble plane, are regard for spiritual values, love of truth and beauty, righteousness, justice and mercy, sympathy with the oppressed and belief in the brotherhood

The Deeper Causes of the War

of man. Any nation or people which separates itself from the rest of the world in the name of race or religion or political creed, and cultivates ideals of conquest by force in order to assert its claims, is not assisting human evolution, but retarding it. Science has made the world one through the facilities of communications and transport now available; and it recognises no political or racial boundaries in its fields of knowledge. Among modern social and intellectual forces it speaks in a tongue which meets with universal understanding and places its achievements at the disposal of the whole world.

The conception of science as a social factor intimately linked up with human history and destiny gives a new meaning to scientific research, and also to the position of citizens who are engaged in it. Both rightly and wrongly, science has been blamed for much of the wastage of life which has been brought about by the rapid application of scientific knowledge to purposes of peace and of war. Men of science are, however, citizens as well as scientific workers; and they are beginning to realise their special responsibilities for making sure that the fruits of scientific knowledge are used for human welfare. They can no longer remain indifferent to the social consequences of discovery and invention, or be silent while they are blamed for increasing powers of production of food supplies, providing means of superseding manual labour by machines and discovering substances which can be used for destructive purposes. It would be a betrayal of the scientific movement if scientific workers failed to

Science and Humane Values

play an active part in solving the social problems which their contributions to natural knowledge have created.

The view that the sole function of science is the discovery and study of natural facts and principles without regard to the social implications of the knowledge gained, can no longer be maintained. It is being widely realised that science cannot be divorced from ethics or rightly absolve itself from the human responsibilities in the application of its discoveries to destructive purposes in war or economic disturbances in times of peace. Men of science cannot continue to stand aside from the social and political questions involved in the structure which has been built up from the materials provided by them, and which their discoveries may be used to destroy. It is their duty to assist in the establishment of a rational and harmonious social order out of the welter of human conflict into which the world has been thrown through the release of uncontrolled sources of industrial production and of lethal weapons.

Science can only continue to render its fullest service to the community as the relations between the general scientific worker and the general citizen are harmonised and the purposes and methods of science are widely understood. In the establishment of such a sympathy, a nobler type of citizenship becomes possible, adequate to defend us against the dangers to which civilisation is exposed and to build a social order on an ethical system worthy of the limitless powers which the increase of natural knowledge has placed in the hands of man.

VII

THE PROBLEM OF AN ORDER OF EUROPE

by

Professor Ernest Barker
LL.D., LITT.D.

THE deeper causes of the war with which I shall be concerned are not the ultimate, but the proximate. If I attempted to analyse the ultimate causes of the war, I should repeat, and I should repeat with admiration, the analysis made by Pius XII in the Encyclical *Summi Pontificatus* which was issued last October. I should say that "the radical and ultimate cause" was "the denial and rejection of a universal norm of morality as well for individual and social life as for international relations." In other words, I should say that the fundamental cause was the rejection of a common rule of life, naturally inherent in man as man (and therefore irrespective of States), and so inherent in virtue of man's allegiance to God. Having said that I should proceed to say, as Pius XII proceeds to say, that two particular errors flow from the primary fault of rejection of a universal norm. The first is the error of forgetting that law of human solidarity and charity which is imposed by the common

The Problem of an Order of Europe

origin of all and the equality of rational nature in all. It is an error which has for its consequence the exaltation of the nation and of the differentia of the nation, and the adoption of the new and abnormal norm that what helps the nation—not what helps humanity—is right. The second error is that of divorcing the authority of civil government from any dependence on a higher law and a greater norm standing above its own will and edicts. It is an error which has for its consequence the claim of civil government to an absolute autonomy and the elevation of the State to a final end and supreme criterion.

I propose to start from this claim of civil government, and this elevation of the State, which is one of the forms or phases of the ultimate cause of the war, and then to pass from it rapidly, as I think I logically can, into the area of what I have called proximate causes.

The governing persons who constitute a civil government readily develop a certain mentality. We may call it, though the word is perhaps too good a word to be properly used in this connection, the mentality of the trustee. They conceive themselves as trustees or agents for an area or space or *Raum*, or, more exactly, for the welfare of the community which occupies· or *should* occupy (that, as we shall see, is the crux) that area or space or *Raum*. Whatever they may individually feel, and whatever may be their private code of morality, they regard themselves as bound—we may even say morally bound—in their official capacity of agent (which is perhaps a better word than "trustee") to do what is demanded by the interest of their community and the area of their community. This constitutes already an "area" norm of morality which may well be different from, and may therefore be in conflict with, the universal norm of morality. Such difference, and such conflict, may emerge internally; in other words, it may show itself in regard to questions concerning the internal position, within the State, of persons or groups of persons. Individuals may be denied rights, under the area norm, which they possess under the universal norm: groups or classes of individuals, such as racial minorities or economic associations or religious communities, may lose rights under the one norm which they enjoy under the other. But the difference and the conflict also emerge externally. Indeed they may be said to emerge particularly in that sphere. The governing persons who constitute a civil government develop the mentality of the trustee—the mentality of the agent—with a particular reference to questions concerning the foreign relations of their State. They begin to ask themselves questions, in their capacity of agent, about the proper area and the proper frontiers of the community included in their State. Transcending the datum of the actual area and the actual frontiers, they make the crucial inquiry (crucial in the sense that it poses the gravest of problems): "What is the area, and what are the frontiers, demanded by the interest of the community?" This is a problem of what ought to be; a problem of the area which a com-

The Problem of an Order of Europe

munity should properly occupy, on the ground of its interest—an interest which the agent conceives himself bound, as agent, to satisfy. It is a problem which leads far afield. Beginning with the question, "What are the frontiers that make the community safe?" the agent glides into the further question, "What are the frontiers that make the community integrated, and recover for it the members of its dispersion?" and from that again he glides into the ultimate question (if indeed it be ultimate), "What is the area, and what are the frontiers, that will enable the community to live a life of well-being in the secure possession of an adequate life-space?"

The development of this mentality, and the raising of these questions, may be said to be permanent features, at any rate hitherto, of the political life of Europe, or at any rate of Central and Eastern Europe. They do not seem to depend on the presence of a particular régime or a particular form of government. Germany has gone through different forms of government during the last eighty years; but whatever the circle of governing persons has been—whether it was the circle round Bismarck, or that round William II, or that now gathered round Hitler—the same sort of mentality, and the same sort of questioning, has emerged. Russia, in 1917, seemed to undergo a total change; but the question which Stalin has raised in Finland is the same sort of question which might have been raised by Peter the Great or the Czar Alexander the First. Faced by this persistence, which seems blindly oblivious of the march of time and of changes in the form of civil government, some thinkers are apt to believe that civil governments generally, and the States (of whatever variety) which are held together by the clamp of civil government, suffer from an inherent vice. They see the State exclusively, or predominantly, in its external aspect: they see it, in that aspect, hungry for domination: and they accordingly tend to regard it as essentially a power-State, concerned by its very nature with dominion rather than justice. Dr. Jacks, for example, in the *Last Legend of Smokeover*, which appeared just before the war, connects the concept of the State with might, dominion and power. It began with the invention of fire-arms and the prosecution of fiery war: it is declining (he hopes) with the invention of the aeroplane and the consequent suicide of war.

This may be called a Hildebrandine frame of mind, which leads the thinker, as Hildebrand himself was led in the opening years of the War of Investitures, to see in governing persons or leaders (*duces*, says Hildebrand, using a word which has a modern flavour) the products of the devil who is the prince of this world and stimulates such persons to affect and pursue dominion. But it may justly be contended that foreign policy, and the aim of the rectification of frontiers by which so much of foreign policy is actuated, is far from being entirely a matter of original sin. The very word "rectification" has its connection with the idea of Right. Nor is that idea alleged merely as an excuse, and as a matter of moral lip-service, to cover action which is intrinsically evil and due

The Problem of an Order of Europe

to evil motives. There is a genuine crux in Central and Eastern Europe. There is a genuine problem of frontiers and boundaries, which is not created, even if it may be exacerbated, by governing persons. Existing States and their existing boundaries are a sort of hard but brittle seal set on moving and heaving populations, animated by ideas of race and nationality, which chafe beneath the seal. Even if we could eliminate governing persons, the problem would still be there. When we do not eliminate them, we must look at them justly, and remember that they are the agents of a problem which they, and we, have to face.

In the issue, therefore, at any rate as regards the proximate causes of the war, we must come down to mother earth, and to the riddles propounded by mother earth in that part of her surface which is called Europe. That is the problem of this war: a problem of Europe, and not of any other continent—a problem not to be solved, as Mr. Clarence K. Streit suggests, by drawing in new worlds to redress the balance of the old—a problem simply and solely, as it stands at present, though it may conceivably widen, of finding an order of Europe. It is a problem, if I may use a Greek word, of *gē*, or what I have just called mother earth: a problem of geology, of geography, of what the Germans call, with a twist or nuance of their own, geopolitics. I have heard it said, and I have more than once repeated the saying, that in the present conjuncture we ought to fix our attention on geology rather than ideology. At any rate geology, the

The Deeper Causes of the War

logos of mother earth—geology in a broad and unscientific sense of the term—shall be my theme.

We are confronted to-day by an unsystematic system of States and political boundaries which is the result of historical contingency, and almost, it may be said, of accident. True, there have been treaties to settle boundaries: true, there was even, in the treaty of 1919, a principle of settlement, the principle of national self-determination. But the present still shows us a congeries which is largely, if not altogether, the result of historical contingency. It is difficult to discover the rationale of this congeries. It is tempting to think of its rationalisation—of some system which would produce rational units of community life, units not deposited by mere historical process, and therefore bearing large traces of a dead and vanished past, but adjusted to our contemporary needs, our contemporary methods of large-scale communications, our contemporary structure of economic production and distribution. "One of the difficulties of our times," if I may quote what I once wrote in another connection, "is that communities formed in one stage of physical and mental communications persist in a different stage." But rationalisation, however tempting it may be, especially on economic grounds, is a dream rather than a possibility. If reason demands rational units, emotion, with all its potency, confronts us with the actual fact of stirring emotional units. The communities deposited by the historical process may occupy areas which are irrational on economic grounds and under the con-

The Problem of an Order of Europe

ditions of our present material civilisation, with its facilities and its needs for large-scale communication. But those communities have acquired, by virtue of that same process, a store of associations and a clustering swarm of emotions. To-day those associations and emotions have acquired, in their turn, the virtue, or the vice, of a lively self-consciousness. With the spread of education, the growth of the Press, the development of broadcasting and the vogue of the film, populations are aware of themselves: they are aware of their boundaries: they cherish a sense of prestige: they are anxious to maintain, or even to extend, the area of their life. The governing persons who are the agents of these communities may help to inspire and inflame their emotion. But there is also a tide in the affairs of men which leads such persons on, to fortune or misfortune.

Germany stands pre-eminent, though she does not stand alone, in this general question of boundaries and this general problem of the area of life which is proper to a community. We may say that the historical process has been harsh to Germany, and that it has done less than justice, in its assignation of areas, to the powers and capacities of the German people. We may also say, and perhaps say with greater truth, that Germany has failed to meet the demands of the historical process, and that by her own internal defects, and through her own internal confusion, she has brought on herself a dispersion of her vital forces, and a circumscription of her area, which is as just a verdict of history as any other

The Deeper Causes of the War

historical verdict. On the one hand, Germany is the great central nation of Europe, looking East and West and North and South. She has become, since the Great Elector began the work in the latter half of the seventeenth century, and the Kings of Prussia carried it forward in the eighteenth and nineteenth centuries, the great military nation of Europe. Since the latter half of the eighteenth century, and from the days of Goethe and Lessing and Kant, she has been able to claim that she is the intellectual nation, though more in the sphere of the speculative than of the practical intellect. From the Middle Ages onwards she has been a colonial nation—we may even say, the great colonial nation of the continent—sending her colonists down the Elbe and the Danube, across to the Vistula, and even as far as the Volga. This is one side of the picture. On the other hand, she dissipated her strength for centuries in internal confusion and foreign adventure. She became lost and entangled in far-flung expansion. New communities, such as Holland, hived off from her: a new and separate Austro-Hungarian Empire ultimately developed out of what had been the old Reich: Germany became a problem to Europe and a problem to herself. There are men still living who were already born when Germany began the Titanic and martial attempt to reverse the results of that historical process which had made her so long a foiled circuitous wanderer. The attempt has already led to five wars for determining the life-space of Germany. What is to be the end?

The Problem of an Order of Europe

But Germany does not stand alone. There is the general problem of Eastern Europe and all its detritus. There is the general problem of Balkan boundaries. From the Gulf of Bothnia to the Black Sea and the Ægean, there are scattered debatable areas. Here is the meeting-ground of Teuton and Slav, and not only of Teuton and Slav, but also of Magyar and Rouman, and indeed of all the peoples who have moved in this region of movement. It is a region in which the lie of the land and the very face of the earth often indicate no boundaries and suggest no natural areas. Is not Poland, by its very name, the land of the level, the country of the illimitable plain? In all this great tract of Europe historical movement, coupled with what may be called geographical indeterminism, has left a series of marks of interrogation. The problem of area and life-space runs from the Rhine to the rivers of Eastern Europe—at any rate as far as the Vistula, the Bug, and the Dniester, which forms the present boundary of Bessarabia.

There are perhaps three main answers which may be given to this problem of area and life-space; three main ways in which an attempt may be made to reshape the results of the historical process. They may all, in their different ways, produce some order of Europe. They differ greatly from one another: at any rate the first of them differs greatly from the last. It is the last to which I wish to give my adhesion; but I will begin by reviewing the other two.

The first answer—the simplest and also the crudest—

The Deeper Causes of the War

is the answer which is given by Germany. She proposes to make a new order of Europe unilaterally and by herself. She proposes to do so on two bases—*Raum* and *Rasse*. Race, at first, bulked largest in her profession: to-day room seems to be prior. On the ground of *Lebensraum* she would clear for herself an area sufficient for her economic needs and adequate to the satisfaction of a growing sense of prestige. But though room may thus seem to be the prior consideration, race returns and asserts its claim. When a sufficient and adequate life-room has been cleared, it will be the domain of a race which feels itself to be a superior and directing race. In the strength of its new and adequate life-room, which may already cover a large and imperial area, the superior and directing race will radiate its influence and establish a general order of Europe based on the potency of that influence. Europe will find itself in clustering round the magnet of Germany.

There are two difficulties in this solution of the problem of an order of Europe. The first and the less fundamental, though it is still a serious difficulty, is that Germany has been forced, in order to clear her Eastern frontier, to adopt a curious coadjutor—a coadjutor with interests which, in the long run, are contrary to the interests of Germany. That coadjutor is Russia; and Russia is the natural barrier to the expansion of German life-space in Eastern and South-Eastern Europe. Even in the improbable event of victory, Germany would still have to reckon with Russia; and unless she proceeded

The Problem of an Order of Europe

to subjugate Russia, she would have established at the best, an uneasy diarchy. But there is a second and more fundamental difficulty in any German solution of the problem of an order of Europe. It would be a unilateral solution, imposed by force: it would be an imperfect solution, because it had no basis in general consent, and because it established a single life-space at the expense of other life-spaces.

A second answer, which is at the antipodes to the German answer, is an answer which is part, though I do not think that it will prove to be the whole, of the allied cause of France and Great Britain. It is an answer which suggests a joint and agreed solution of the problem of boundaries and areas, by which each community would secure an internationally determined life-space. In this sense, our own Prime Minister, in his broadcast speech of November 26th, suggested that "Such adjustments of boundaries as would be necessary would be thrashed out between neighbours sitting on equal terms round a table with the help of disinterested third parties if it were so desired." Such a policy must necessarily be followed in the event of an allied victory, as a part—but again I repeat that I think it can only be a part—of a general settlement. The Czech people must find an area: the Polish people must find an area: the people of Austria must have a liberty of option, and must freely decide whether they wish to have an area of their own, or whether they wish to join another area, and, if so, on what conditions. But such a settlement, if it stood by

The Deeper Causes of the War

itself, would soon be exposed to what I may call revisionism, which in turn would be the parent, as revisionism so often is, of another war.

Each great European settlement has been exposed to revisionism. The settlement of Utrecht, in 1713, was followed by it: the settlement of Vienna, in 1815, was followed by it: the settlement of Versailles, in 1919, was followed by it. Is Europe to be the perpetual prey of settlement, revisionism, war—settlement, revisionism, war—in a recurrent and unending cycle? Surely we must all profoundly desire the contrary.

I am thus brought to the third answer which may be given to the problem of an order of Europe. It is an answer which is in no way contradictory to the second: it is rather an answer which has to be added to the second. It is the answer which is generally called federalism. But we must beware of using the word federalism as a magic key which will easily unlock the dark door of the future. European federalism is a thing of difficulty, and indeed of very great difficulty. But it has the merit of going to the root of the problem of areas and boundaries, and, if it can be achieved, of providing a solution of that problem which may well prove to be permanent.

Let us begin by noticing that the two last great European settlements were both of them attended by a general scheme which was added to the settlement of areas and boundaries. The settlement of 1815 was attended by the scheme of the Concert of Europe: the

The Problem of an Order of Europe

settlement of 1919 was attended by the scheme of the League of Nations. But each of these schemes, while it attempted some form of unity—in the one case a European form; in the other, and perhaps prematurely, an oecumenical or world form—none the less left the plenarily autonomous State as the basis of such unity.

That was the essence, and that was the danger, of both schemes. If you leave the plenarily autonomous State as your basis, you leave unextracted the sting, the essential sting, which exacerbates the problem of boundaries and areas. Whatever your scheme of unity, you leave at its restless work the moving stimulus of autonomy—the zest of an entire and plenary self-direction which naturally, and almost inevitably, at any rate under the conditions of Central and Eastern Europe, becomes plenary self-expansion. The real question, the question of questions, is whether you can extract the sting.

This is the question before Europe. I cannot but feel that as long as we move in terms of the plenarily autonomous State we also move in terms of boundary-questions, area-questions, and a restless expansionism. The two things are psychologically connected: the frame of mind connected with the first necessarily carries, and necessarily entails, the frame of mind connected with the second. In the same way I cannot but feel that a State which resigns and discards some of the sting of plenary autonomy, which is also called national sovereignty—a State which writes a minus against national

The Deeper Causes of the War

sovereignty, first in this respect, and then in that, and then again in that—such a State will be a State which has necessarily a different frame of mind in respect to boundaries and areas and the possibilities of expansion. It will not be thinking entirely of itself. It will have other and additional interests outside itself—the interests of the new order and system to which it has resigned some portion or portions of its sovereignty. It will feel that, whatever its own immediate area, and even if that area seems imperfect, there is another and compensating greater area in which it is included and which it can help to move and determine. A new psychological condition emerges from such conditions.

An objection occurs to this line of argument which is a great and serious objection. It may be urged that we are putting the cart before the horse. In other words, it may be said that we are arguing that the resignation of some portion or portions of national sovereignty will ease the problem of boundaries, when the case is really the other way round, and some easing or settlement of the problem of boundaries is really the prior condition of any resignation of any portion of national sovereignty. It may also be contended, and contended even more drastically, that whether or no there is any prior easing or settlement of the problem of boundaries, national sovereignty is the last thing in the world of which a single iota is ever likely to be resigned.

I should not deny the weight of such objections. I should admit that the easing of the problem of boundaries

The Problem of an Order of Europe

has to go hand in hand with the resignation of some elements of sovereignty, and I should settle the question of priority by saying that, on a short-time view and under present conditions, the cart and the horse must move side by side. On a long-time view I should still contend that the resignation of some portion or portions of sovereignty is the prior or more important thing, which alone can prevent the problem of boundaries from being an eternal problem of blood and war. And I should also contend that to despair of any voluntary and gradual diminution of sovereignty is to despair of the whole of the future, and to despair, too, at a time when the signs of the times are set in the very opposite direction. France and Great Britain have recently resigned to one another—or rather to institutions above them both, such as the Supreme War Council and the Anglo-French Co-ordinating Committee—some portion of their national sovereignty. True, it has been done in war, and not in peace. True, again, it has been done between two States, and only two States; but most of us, again, are already asking why it should not be done between more States than two, and why a common need, not peculiar to France and Great Britain, should not produce a common union.

I have confined myself, in these remarks, to the philosophy of the State, if there be such a philosophy. I have confined myself accordingly to what I called at the beginning the proximate causes of the war. I have suggested that the great proximate cause is geology

The Deeper Causes of the War

rather than ideology; but I have also suggested that the geological problem of boundaries and areas and life-spaces is connected with a conception of the State, which, as we are becoming increasingly aware, stands in need of modification. I have accepted, and put before you, that line of modification which is already, as I see the matter, being tentatively pursued, and to which many minds are already giving their adhesion. Let me end by repeating what I have already indicated, and what indeed is suggested by the title of my paper. The problem before us is a problem of the order of Europe—not more, and also not less. As a problem of the order of Europe, and not more than that problem, it does not concern, in my view, the United States of America—at any rate immediately, and unless we should fail by our own resources to find a solution ourselves. That is why I am not a disciple of Mr. Streit's *Union Now*. But as a problem of the order of Europe, and not less than that problem, it is a very great and a very grave concern. It concerns all Europe—all its States, at any rate to the borders of Russia; all its States, and all the individuals living in those States; and so far as Europe concerns the world, and the peace of Europe helps the peace of the world, it concerns the world.

Seeing how great and how grave a concern is involved, we shall also see that a federal union between the States of Europe is not the whole of the matter. A union or arrangement between European States is a beginning. But it is just a beginning. Other questions arise, and

The Problem of an Order of Europe

indeed are already being asked. I will mention two as I end, and leave you to think about them. First, is there to be a European standard of civilisation common to all federated States, if a system of federated States should actually arise? Is there to be a declaration of rights, to which all States shall subscribe? I said, a moment ago, that this great and grave concern was a concern of all individuals as well as of all States. Can the individual be guaranteed the conditions of a common norm and the enjoyment of a common standard expressed in terms of rights? This is a question which Mr. H. G. Wells and others have raised; and it is a question which has to be faced. Secondly, and perhaps no less solemn, there is the question of the relation of a federal order of Europe, if such an order should be established, to the scheme of the League of Nations. How shall that relation be conceived? I cannot conceive that a new European order would make the existing scheme of world-order otiose. On the contrary, I believe that it would make that scheme more necessary than ever. But it may vitally affect and vitally modify the present plan of that scheme. A reconstruction of the League of Nations, partly based on twenty years' experience of trial and error, but partly also based on the new fact of a new order of Europe, may well be the work of the next generation. Schemes of reconstruction are already being ventilated. The time for their realisation is not yet; but I hope and pray that I may live to see the beginning of the work.

III

PEACE BY FEDERATION?

by

Sir William Beveridge

K.C.B., B.C.L., F.B.A.

In a world already darkened by wars, the problem of world order can be approached in two ways—general and special. Generally, we may examine the causes of war, the possible types of relation between nations, and the means for securing that disputes between them are settled by pacific means. Specially, we may consider the origins and circumstances of a particular war now in progress, the probable conditions of its ending, and the terms of settlement which are most likely both to prevent a repetition of that war and to lay foundations of permanent and general peace. No excuse is needed for choosing in this paper the second line of approach, through consideration of the war in which Britain and her allies are now engaged against Germany. This approach means examining the problem of world order in the first instance from the point of view of a particular group of nations—Britain and her allies—but that is the natural point of view for a British writer. It need not involve inability at a later stage to correct the national

Peace by Federation?

equation of the writer by reference to wider interests. It has the advantage of practicality. The foundations of world order must be laid on facts, on the geography, economics, and psychology of particular nations, rather than on reasoning about nations in general.

Choice of this line of approach involves a particular point of view, to be widened later. It involves also two assumptions which should be stated. One assumption is that, in ending this war, Britain and her allies will find themselves in a position to secure, either by dictation or by agreement, peace terms of the kind that they desire; if this cannot be assumed, the writing of pamphlets on world order is irrational. Another assumption is that Britain and her allies desire and will continue to desire in making peace, not to end this war only, but to stamp out the seeds of future war.

The actual approach to peace, as it unfolds itself from the events of war in the months or years that lie ahead, may look very different from these assumptions. To contemplate defeat for the allied nations in their own borders is unprofitable as well as unjustified pessimism. But if the war is prolonged there will come hints of peace and offers of mediation, reflecting the shifting balance of military events. There may come chances of securing by agreement without victory what looks like nearly all the Allies want but may be something far short of it. There may come periods of frustration, when, as in 1916, the Allied leaders find themselves weighing possible gains by continuing the

The Deeper Causes of the War

war against the certain relief of stopping it, will be setting hope of release from bloodshed for unknown future generations against the lives of the generation that they know. In 1916 the decision to continue was sustained by hope of a final settlement with war itself. In November 1918 these hopes seemed to be realized. In the mood of 1919, when nearly all the great nations of the world were exhausted by war or hating it with passion, it seemed possible, and it was taken as a practical aim, to banish war for ever from the earth. The basic assumption of this paper is the aim, if not the mood, of 1919.

THE BRITISH COMMONWEALTH, FRANCE AND GERMANY

"It is . . . comparatively easy to patch up a peace which will last for thirty years; what is difficult . . . is to draw up a peace which will not provoke a fresh struggle when those who have had practical experience of what war means have passed away."[1] So wrote Mr. Lloyd George on March 25, 1919, in a memorandum designed to resist the desire of the French for a military frontier on the Rhine and in place thereof to base on justice a peace that should be permanent.

The memorandum achieved its immediate object. The plan of Marshal Foch for establishing the Rhine as a barrier against German attack was rejected. The Treaty of Versailles was signed on June 28, 1919. The peace thus established has lasted just twenty years, not

[1] *The Truth About the Peace Treaties*, vol. i, p. 404.

Peace by Federation?

thirty years, not an eternity. What are the reasons for this tragic defeat of expectations? What lessons should be drawn from it for guidance in the future?

One view is that in 1919 Marshal Foch was right and Mr. Lloyd George was wrong—that the Treaty of Versailles erred, not by excessive severity of the terms imposed upon the beaten enemy, but through their weakness. If we ask, however, whether a military frontier on the Rhine would have guaranteed the peace of Europe, the question, in 1940, is answered in the negative as soon as it is asked. A barrier on the Rhine would have been irrelevant to the defence of Czecho-Slovakia or Poland—or Britain or Roumania. A barrier on the Rhine is no barrier to aircraft; one cannot build a Maginot Line 20,000 feet high in the air.

Another and commoner view is that the Treaty of Versailles failed through its injustice and vindictiveness. That Treaty contains some features, such as reparations and the war guilt clause, which few people would defend to-day. It contains provisions as to colonies which nothing but casuistry can seek to reconcile with the Armistice terms. But it does not deserve one-tenth of the facile abuse that has been heaped upon it. The worst inequities of the last war settlement, such as the failure to implement minority provisions, and the Italo-Austrian border, are no part of the Treaty of Versailles. The boundaries drawn elsewhere than on the Brenner Pass might easily have been much the same, if they had been the subject of adjudication by an impartial tribunal

The Deeper Causes of the War

after hearing all parties, in place of being dictated by Allied and Associated Powers. More than this, the Treaty of Versailles contained a genuine attempt to establish a new world order and to enthrone justice in place of war as the arbiter amongst nations.

The plan of 1919 for this purpose failed completely, less through lack of will than through lack of knowledge, through failure to understand the new conditions of peace in Europe and the changes of old habits and institutions that were required to secure it. If to the passionate desire for peace that filled the world in 1919 we could add the experience of the past twenty years, what should be now proposed? What are the real lessons of those years?

The first lesson, which it would be foolish to ignore and dishonest to conceal with false-friendly phrases, is that there can be no assurance of peace with justice in Europe so long as the German people can have arms at their discretion. This is not the whole truth about national armaments, but it is true and lies at the root of the European problem. The powers of organisation and discipline of this highly talented and numerous people in a central situation in Europe, combined with their readiness to hand over their destinies, time and again, to leaders whose creed is power, leave no other conclusion possible than that the condition of permanent peace in Europe is permanent disarmament of Germany.

How and on what terms can the permanent disarmament of Germany be secured?

Peace by Federation?

One plan has been tried already in 1919—enforced unilateral disarmament of Germany coupled with promises by other nations (under the fourth of the Fourteen Points) to reduce their arms "to the lowest point consistent with domestic safety." Under this plan most nations other than Germany remained heavily armed, yet the nations most concerned—Britain and France—failed to stop re-armament of Germany. Between 1934 and 1938 the world received an impressive demonstration of the unwillingness of the British and French democracies to fight on an uneasy conscience or to look ahead. It may be said that such lethargy would not be repeated. If Germany could once again be disarmed by victorious democracies, even the democracies could be trusted to keep her disarmed for ever. The Foch prescription of military occupation of the Rhine would be converted into military domination.

Already voices are being raised, in this country and in France, urging that their peace aim should be to break up Germany once more. "Mr. Chamberlain talks of lasting guarantees. There is only one: the destruction of German unity. Left to herself, Germany will always produce Hitlers" (M. André Chaumeix in *Paris Soir*, October 14, 1939). The Allies should declare that they "will not discuss peace except with the historical or elected representatives of the twenty-five states comprised in the Germany of 1866" (M. Charles Maurras in *Action Française*, October 11, 1939). " 'With malice towards none' of the German peoples—to use Abraham Lincoln's great words—there is probably only one way to safeguard Europe. That is to reconstitute the old German kingdoms and principalities, if necessary under some measure of control and supervision by their several neighbours; the creation, possibly, of a Catholic South-German and Austrian State, which would be unlikely to coalesce with its northern Protestant neighbours; and, in fact, the re-establishment of the Germanies, which for centuries constituted no danger to Europe before their absorption into a single entity began under the leadership of Prussia." (General Dawnay in *The Times*, December 1, 1939.)

If the German people should themselves come to desire disunion and impotence in a world of arms, it would be reasonable to accede to their desire. But we cannot put the clock back seventy years by force and keep it back except by continuing force.

I do not believe that a peace plan of this nature would commend itself to public opinion in Britain at any time, or to enduring public opinion in France; it would be rejected by the rest of the world. In any case it is impracticable and out of date. In 1919 it was possible to think of German disarmament as a prelude to general disarmament; there had been a world war making a world weary of war. The conflict to-day is limited and may remain limited. However it ends, however weary of war the principal belligerents may be, there will be other nations in Europe, not exhausted

Peace by Federation?

by war, not ready to disarm. Above all, there will be Russia. All plans for merely reducing Germany to impotence, by disarmament or by forcible disunion, ignore one of the main elements in the situation—the Russian Revolution. They involve a permanent military occupation of all Germany in force sufficient both to keep Germany down and to keep Russia out, Russia and the Comintern.

To say this is not to take sides in the dispute between socialism and capitalism, planned or other, as methods for organising the economic activities of mankind. Socialism is consistent with preservation of essential liberties and is consistent with peace and justice between nations. If socialism were ever established in Britain by the will of the people, it would not make the citizen less free in essentials or threaten other nations with war. But Soviet Communism to-day is another thing altogether —a tyranny which makes many Socialists feel that Socialism is not worth the Russian price, a tyranny become as shameless in aggression as Hitlerism itself. To-day the one redeeming virtue of Soviet Communism in the eyes of other nations is its probable inefficiency in organising war. This virtue would not be found in Communism of like spirit established in Germany. By the sacrifice of millions of lives from 1914 to 1918 the Allied and Associated Powers exorcised hereditary militant autocracy from Germany, and made a home for Hitlerism. If now Britain and France are able to exorcise Hitlerism, but do no more, they will leave a land swept

The Deeper Causes of the War

clear of hope and garnished with hate, a fit dwelling for a worse spirit still.

The French feel, with justice, that in 1919 they were cheated of security. They will want on this occasion, if they can, as the British will want, to be done with danger from Germany once and for all. They will not think that they are done with danger, merely through a change of government in Germany. "Hitler made the war, but the Germans made Hitler." "Germany left to herself will always produce Hitlers." Those are typical summings up of the situation in the French press and it is difficult to deny their justice. The French people in M. Daladier's words, will not on this occasion lay down their arms without "material guarantees" against German aggression in the future. They ought not to be asked to do so, by the British or by anyone else.

But "material guarantees" are not to be found in merely reducing Germany to impotence. They have to be sought, rather, along another line, also indicated by a distinguished leader of French opinion, M. Léon Blum. The material guarantees for the security and peace of other nations in Europe are to be sought through "the integration of Germany into a European system." What M. Blum had in mind in this phrase is shown by another passage written by him a few days before: "The independence and security of peoples in a federated and disarmed Europe must be guaranteed."[1] More recently the French Prime Minister, M. Daladier, has

[1] *Populaire*, October 14 and 10, 1939.

Peace by Federation?

said: "It will be necessary . . . perhaps to envisage federal ties between the various States of Europe."[1]

These leaders of French opinion point the way in which the world should move. Before following their thought to its practical conclusion it will be useful to survey the problem from a wider point of view than that of Britain and her allies.

AS OTHERS SEE IT

Britain and France in their own view are peace-loving nations, reluctantly at war after every effort at conciliation had failed, defending themselves but defending also the common interest of all nations against a treacherous and dangerous enemy of mankind. This view is not baseless, but it is over-simple.

First, to the British and the French, though perhaps not to them only, German arms appear to be the most dangerous arms in the world. But they are not the only national armaments which threaten peace and justice among nations. Other nations are equally aggressive, equally ready to use war as an instrument of national policy, equally unwilling to submit their disputes to conciliation or arbitration; their arms are less dangerous to peace than German arms only because they are less efficient in war. And though to-day the British and French feel themselves to be full of sweet reason and pillars of international justice, the earlier record of these

[1] December 29, 1939, in a speech to Senate.

The Deeper Causes of the War

countries, when from 1919 to 1932 their arms dominated the world, does not bear examination. The Reparation and Colonies clauses of the Versailles Treaty in 1919, the occupation of the Ruhr in 1923 and the prohibition of the economic union of Austria with Germany in 1932, were indefensible mis-uses of power. No nation can be trusted to be judge in its own cause.

Second, national armaments as such, not German armaments alone, are both the condition of war (there could be no mass-killing by nations if they had no means of killing) and a common cause of war. The war of 1914–18 was the product of armaments plus fear, as that of 1939 has been largely the product of armaments plus sense of national wrong. The wrong itself, or one element in it—the seizure of German colonies—was the product of fear of armament.

Third, though the British and French peoples to-day are pacific, they do not realise what makes them so. There is no need to prove with many words the pacific character of Britain and France to-day; it shines in their actions and inactions. Whatever mistakes of policy or injustices may be charged to the earlier record of these two nations, they have given from 1934 to 1938 proofs of a passionate desire for peace. So long as Germany was doing only what Britain and France would have claimed a right to do in their own case—fortifying her own territory, absorbing willing German populations into the new German Reich—they accepted these actions, even when undertaken in breach of free

Peace by Federation?

recent agreements or assurances. They stood by, ready to make fresh agreements; they made war only when the banditry of the Nazi régime had been unmasked thrice over. The people of Britain and France are as pacific as those of the United States of America. But none of these nations appreciates the reason for their love of peace, as it appears to others; all three nations cause natural irritation by assuming that their love of peace is due to their superior morality. To others it has a simpler explanation. In the genial philosophy of dictators, small nations are peaceable because they are afraid, and large nations are peaceable (if they are peaceable) only because there is nothing more for them to get by war. The great democracies, as seen by the dictators of Germany and Italy and pictured to the German and Italian people, are peaceful as the rich are conservative, because they are satisfied; they control territories ample for their populations and rich in raw materials. Britain, in particular, according to a frequent gibe of Herr Hitler, has become virtuous only after two hundred years of successful wickedness. German propaganda in the present war is marked by alignment of attack upon Britain as both imperialist and plutocratic; Nazi Socialism carries the banner of the disinherited nations and classes. The picture is grotesque but informing. In the view of their rulers, Germany and Italy, coming to unity and power after other nations have carved the world to their satisfaction, cannot be expected to show the same attitude or to be blind devotees of peace.

The Deeper Causes of the War

Germany and Italy are "dissatisfied" powers needing for their people territories and opportunities now held by others; if they cannot get these by agreement, they are entitled and bound to seek them by war.

It is easy to find argumentative answers to this case. The view popular with the victors of 1918, that democracies as such are more peaceable than autocracies, is not without justification, however unpopular it may be outside the democracies. The general international argument against dictators is strong and has been strengthened by recent happenings. The specific claims of Germany and of Italy alike are riddled by weakness. Both, for instance, signed under no compulsion the Paris Pact, renouncing war as an instrument of national policy; both show by their recent acts that they meant nothing by these signatures. Both, again, while declaring that they have insufficient living room for their nationals are feverishly attempting to raise their birth-rates and increase the number of their nationals. Finally, the German case for return of her colonies has no economic justification; her trade with them has always been insignificant; emigration to them from Germany has been trifling. The significance of her former colonies to Germany is strategic; they would have provided bases from which to organise success in war and win other colonies. The significance of Germany's claim for free access to raw materials is much the same; she has not been denied access in peace; the sting lies in not being able to get materials in war.

Peace by Federation?

All this is true but does not meet the issue. Argumentative answers without understanding breed counter-argument and irritation, not conviction and peace.

Granted that dictatorships are more likely than democracies to lead to war, what leads to dictatorships? Historically, the Nazi dictatorship is the channel through which the German people have expressed their sense of economic suffering and national injustice. Germany must ultimately be made peaceful in accord with her own desires and not against them. She must be allowed to share the economic opportunities which in her view make peace easy for the democracies.

"Left to herself, Germany will always produce Hitlers." She cannot be left to herself. Germany cannot be allowed to have arms of her own, if Europe is to have security, but she cannot be left unarmed. There must be arms to protect Germany; ultimately, if not forthwith, they must be arms shared by her with others. She must be integrated into a European system—on the terms not of servitude but of partnership. When Germany is ready to return to civilization, she must be embraced, not as an enemy, but as a friend.

Europe in many American eyes is a prize-ring. After each round the victor of that round has gone about his business; the loser, left in his corner, has nursed himself back to strength and vengeance in the next round. Wars so ended settle nothing. But in earlier stages of human history wars might settle things; they might end in conquest which is one way to lasting peace. The third course, the way of the future, superseding both conquest and the prize-ring, is partnership. If the present war is to end by laying the foundations of international order in Europe, it must end by a union in which Britain, France and Germany shall at last make war between them impossible for ever. Peace must come by their federation.

A PEACE FEDERATION

Federalism is not new in the world or in the experience of Britons: the United States of America, Switzerland, Canada, Australia, are federations of proved success. The new departure now proposed in world government is federation across long established national boundaries.

On any such proposal three questions arise at the outset. What nation-states should be included in the federation? What should be the division of powers between the federal and the national governments? What should be the form of the federal government? Needless to say, these questions cannot be answered fully here. Nor are the answers given put forward dogmatically; they are intended only to illustrate the nature and purpose of the main proposal.

States for Inclusion

First, as to the States to be included. The proposal for federation in this paper is a peace proposal, designed in ending the present war to establish a barrier against

Peace by Federation?

future wars. It is a "Peace Federation" and the States envisaged as its members are all those who as belligerents or as neutrals have been most deeply concerned in the present war and will have suffered by it. This means in Europe, Britain, France and Germany as belligerents, Denmark, Norway, Sweden, Finland, Belgium, Holland, Switzerland, and Eire as neutrals; it means, outside Europe, the four self-governing Dominions of the British Commonwealth who are belligerent—Australia, Canada, New Zealand, and South Africa. The treatment of Poland and Czecho-Slovakia, when they are restored, depends upon other possible groupings in Europe.

The following comments explain the choice of countries for federation:

(*a*) The area is limited and therefore manageable. The federal principle is not now, if it ever will be, applicable to world government. The States suggested have a population of 235,000,000 in a total area of 8,822,000 square miles. This is a little more than the U.S.S.R. in area and about a third greater in population. It is rather more than twice the area of the U.S.A. and rather less than twice the population. With the exception of the British Dominions (considered specially below) the States are contiguous to one another.

(*b*) The States have to a large extent a common culture, comparable standards of life, close economic relations, and all but one of them is already democratic. The exception—Germany—has been democratic from 1919 to 1933 and before 1914 had a strong and growing democratic movement. As is explained below, practical considerations of government make it necessary to limit federation to effective democracies, i.e. to exclude dictatorships and one-party States.

(*c*) The inclusion of Germany is essential to making the federation an organ of assured peace. If she is in, the neighbouring neutrals will have every reason for coming in, for certain security. Without Germany, the federation will look too much like an alliance against fascist States. The adhesion of the neutrals is important for two reasons. First, they will hold the balance of power in the federal government between those who are now belligerent. Second, as small nations, they take naturally the right view of human values; they pursue the happiness of the common people because they cannot provide glory for rulers.

(*d*) The inclusion of the four British Dominions and Eire, while not essential, is highly desirable. Clearly Britain could not go into a European federation turning her back upon the British Commonwealth. She could not enter herself except after full consultation with the self-governing Dominions and regard for their views; if they were not willing to join but Britain did join, she would have to preserve a special relation to them. But their experience in the working of democratic and federal institutions would be invaluable; two of them—Canada and South Africa—already combine populations of different European origins; some at least would continue to need the security against other powers that

Peace by Federation?

federal membership would secure. The geographical position of the Dominions, outside Europe, might be a reason for admitting them on special terms, e.g. with a recognized right of secession not accorded to others. But their position outside Europe is another reason for bringing them into the suggested federation if possible. The federation is a federation in the world, not outside the world; a step towards world order and co-operation, not a move towards isolation.

(e) The relation of India to the federation raises a special problem. Negatively it is clear that India could not be brought into the federation as an additional State on the same terms as the rest without changing its character. India is of Asia, not of Europe or of Europe exported to other continents; she is large enough and populous enough to require federation on her own account. The logical immediate answer on the problem of India is to say that the federation would stand to India in whatever relation Britain stood at the time when Britain joined the federation; whatever responsibilities for external defence or internal order of India remained to Britain then would be undertaken by the federation. But it would be equally possible for Britain within the federation to maintain special relations with India and the means of giving effect to them.

Division of Powers

In regard to the division of powers between federal and national government, this should follow the American plan of giving named powers to the federal government and leaving to the national governments everything that is neither transferred to the federal government, nor reserved to the people by constitutional guarantees. The problem is thus one of defining what powers shall be transferred to the federal government as dealing with "common affairs." The answer is best given in three stages.

(a) *Defence and Foreign Policy.*—Two affairs are certainly common and form the minimum for transfer, viz. defence and foreign policy. This means, in the end, that all the armed forces of all the federated nations will become a single force, owing allegiance to the federal government and not to the national governments. There will be no *British* Navy, no *German* Army, no *French* Air Force, but British, German, French, Swedish, Belgian and other contingents of a federal navy, army and air force.

To many this will be a hard saying—at first, perhaps, too hard to be accepted. Those who find pooling of all arms in a federation unthinkable must face the alternatives. Is it worth while to keep a British Navy at cost of there being a German Army and a German Air Force? Is it feasible to keep British and French armaments while denying them to others? That was tried in 1919, with results known to all. If Britain and her allies were once again in the dominant position of 1919, there would be temptation to ensure security for themselves by their own arms. Could they trust themselves, would they be

Peace by Federation?

trusted by others, not to abuse power, not to use it for economic gain? An alternative of another type is that one form of armed force—say that of the air—should be made international or super-national, while other forms remain under national control. It is difficult to see merit in such a compromise. If the force which remains national is of a scale and type that it can challenge the super-national force, it may become the basis of aggressive civil war. If not, it is a delusive safeguard; it makes armed conflict and bloodshed possible for no advantage.

The steps by which the pooling of the armed forces of an international federation could be brought about depend on the circumstances in which the federation came to birth. The military aspects of accomplished federation need expert consideration. But if the peoples wish to get security through federation, it is hard to suppose that the military problem of guaranteeing their security against civil war would prove insoluble. Critics of federation often cite the American Civil War as proof that federation may fail to prevent war between member states. The reply to this criticism is that the American Civil War occurred seventy-five years ago, and that since that time there have been two revolutions—one in arms and one in the minds of men. First, in the America of 1860 the simple arms required were available to all; every man had his musket. The aeroplanes, tanks, submarines and scientific equipment of modern warfare are not broadcast and cannot be improvised. So simple a device as making guns in one part of the federation and

The Deeper Causes of the War

the shells to fit them in another part might prove an effective safeguard against revolution or forcible secession. Second, war, in the minds of all peoples who know it, bears an aspect to-day very different from its aspect even a generation ago: to talk of civilised man as a fighting animal, when fighting means modern totalitarian war, is patently ridiculous. War threatens to die of inanition in the minds of thoughtful men. The greatest danger to civilisation to-day is not the risk that war will go on for ever, but that the more civilised nations will abandon war too soon, before others do, and will leave the world to the oppressors.

The ordinary citizen to-day does not have to be kept from fighting; the ordinary citizen to-morrow, fresh from new experience of war, will be ready to barter arms for security. The men of the fighting professions will not find anything unthinkable in federation. The traditions and spirit of those who, in different nations choose, the risks of the fighting professions have much in common. The British Navy becoming, as at first it naturally would be, the main part of a federal navy, would find no difficulty in keeping the peace of the seas with a wider loyalty.

(*b*) *Dependencies*.—Control of dependencies is common up to a certain point, though not necessarily to the full extent of transfer of all dependencies to the federal government for direct administration by a federal Civil Service. The treatment of dependencies raises many problems both of principle and of technique. It involves

Peace by Federation?

consideration of interests other than those of the federal States, namely, the native populations, and States outside the federation. The dependencies themselves are various. The policies hitherto adopted by the chief colonial Powers which may become members of the federation—Britain and the Dominions, France, Belgium and Holland—are different. Finally, the question of what should be done about colonies to-day is complicated by a troubled past.

Under the fifth of President Wilson's Fourteen Points there was to be "a free, open-handed and absolutely impartial adjustment of all colonial claims, based upon strict observance of the principle that in determining all such questions of sovereignty the interests of the population concerned must have equal weight with the equitable claims of the Government whose title is to be determined." Under the Treaty of Versailles all the German colonies were transferred without consultation with Germany or with their inhabitants as mandates to Powers other than Germany. There is no point in the whole Treaty which is harder to reconcile with the Fourteen Points.

It is true that the Point quoted above, in spite of its length and elaboration, gives no guidance as to how the "equitable claims" of more than one Government claiming sovereignty over a colony were to be weighed, not against the interests of the inhabitants, but against one another. It is true also that the author of the Point in due course signed the Treaty. But the Fourteen Points

The Deeper Causes of the War

were addressed to Germany, as an invitation to lay down arms. No one could then have expected her to believe that she would have no opportunity of putting forward any colonial claims at all; no one can describe the action of the Allied and Associated Powers in regard to the German colonies as "open-handed."

The plain fact is that in preliminary discussion at Paris those Allied and Associated Powers whose territory lay anywhere near the German colonies were not prepared to see the colonies return into the hands of a Power which might use them as war bases to threaten oversea communications. Breach of faith with the Fourteen Points was dictated by fear of German armaments in the future. Very few people will be sorry to-day that these Powers, chiefly the British Dominions, had their way; a British Commonwealth which of its own will allowed Germany to possess both colonies and independent arms would be graduating for suicide. But the colonial clauses are a heavy count in Germany's hostility to Britain and in the world's judgment on the treaty-makers of Versailles. There is something here to be set right in the next treaty.

But it cannot be set right on the old lines. No British interest in Tanganyika is worth a war in Europe. But the principle that millions of human beings should not be transferred, without regard either to their wishes or to their interests, from one government to another, that they should not be treated as bargaining counters by others, is worth a war; in application to Poland that principle is the cause and justification of the war in which

Peace by Federation?

Britain and her Allies are now engaged. The problem of dependencies must be solved by looking to the future, not to the past.

Dependencies are communities in which the force necessary for order, both internal and external, is applied from outside. It is legitimate to apply force in that way if order cannot be assured without it; it is illegitimate to apply force, in war or in peace, to secure special economic advantage for the holder of force, or indeed for any other purpose than the advantage common to all, of security in which the citizens of all countries can pursue their peaceful avocations.

The principle of the future is that the aim of colonial administration is to prepare the inhabitants of each dependency to become full citizens of the modern world, and that meanwhile, till this preparation issues in self-government, the interests of the native inhabitants must be paramount. Britain has not acted on this principle invariably in the past. But it was adopted for her by the British Secretary of State in June 1939.[1] The treatment of dependencies under federation should be that which will go farthest towards securing application of this principle everywhere and at all times. If it were certain that the Peace Federation as a whole would adopt this principle, for all dependencies within its scope, that would be a reason for making the administration of dependencies wholly a federal affair; thereby the troubled past of the colonial problem would be laid to rest most simply.

[1] *Hansard*, June 7, 1939.

The Deeper Causes of the War

With the varied policies favoured by different colonial Powers hitherto, this happy conclusion is not certain. It may be that an alternative plan, leaving the administration of all or most dependencies with national governments, while giving the federal government powers of supervision and control, will be preferable in practice. But clearly the federal powers would need to be much greater than those now accorded to the Mandates Commission of the League of Nations. They would extend to all dependencies. They would have to secure effectively three aims: (*a*) the paramountcy of native interests; (*b*) equality among all citizens of member States for trading access and settlement; (*c*) fair consideration of the interests of States outside the federation. They might provide for recruiting all or some of the branches of the Civil Service, even under national administration, from different nations. They might place in the hands of the federal government the substantial funds that will be required for colonial development—a small fraction of its savings on internecine armaments, turned into a means of influence as grants in aid. Whatever be done at the outset, the part of the federal government here is bound to grow. The problem of dependencies is a world problem. Discussion of that problem with States outside the Peace Federation must be a federal affair.

(*c*) *Currency, Trade, Migration.*—There remains as the third stage of discussion, the problem of economic affairs. Should any of these be regarded as common and transferred to the federal authority, or should they all

Peace by Federation?

be left to the national authorities? This raises technical questions of great complexity on which no final answer can be given.

Mr. Clarence Streit, in his projected federation of fifteen democracies including the United States, contemplates within this area a single currency and absolute freedom of trade and migration. It may be doubted whether all the practical consequences of this proposal have been envisaged by him, in relation to the financial and economic systems of the countries concerned and their differing standards of wages. It is probably wiser to assume that even if currency, trade and migration were treated as common affairs, so that the federal authority had power to deal with them, the authority would decide that some barriers and differences between the separate states should continue at least for a period.

The question of how much economic power should be given to the federal authority is essentially a question of how far the different nations are prepared to go towards unity. Very considerable transfer of economic powers from the national to the federal authority—extending to final control over currency, trade and migration—is probably the ideal. Economic activities are already to a large extent international. Economic problems, such as cyclical fluctuation of trade, are common and call for international or super-national solutions. Foreign policy in the modern world is largely concerned with economics; it is difficult to envisage a federal authority unable to negotiate commercial treaties with States outside the federation, but every such negotiation involves the economic interests of one or more member-states. The federal authority will have a stronger hold on the loyalty of all its citizens and will grow in the unity which makes strength, if it has common constructive tasks of peace, not merely armaments and foreign policy within its sphere. Finally, the federation may be brought together as an escape from war. It must be kept together by conferring economic benefits which no State will desire to relinquish by secession; that it can confer such benefits need not be doubted.

The issue is one of the feeling of the nations when they come together in federation. It is better that they should federate for defence and foreign policy and equal access to their dependencies than not at all. They may come together more easily on a limited programme. But the further they can go in economic co-operation even at the outset, the stronger will be the bonds that will always unite them.

There will remain in any case a large field for national activity and distinctions, in education, health, social services and local administration, in forms and machinery of state government, in ways of living and ways of thought. In discussing the federation of nation-states it is natural to say most about those functions which might become federal. They have to be named because it is practically certain that division of powers in this case would follow the American and Australian precedents rather than the Canadian precedent; the federal authority

Peace by Federation?

would have defined powers while an undefined residue would be left to national authorities. But the ordinary citizen as a rule would be more conscious of the national than of the federal government.

Form of Federal Authority

In regard to the form of the federal authority, the framing of this is governed by two general considerations—that the individualities of the member states, large and small, must be adequately protected, and that the federal authority must be strong, with unquestioned power in its own sphere.

The first of these general considerations is important both for acceptance of federation at the outset, and for keeping it together in contentment. The purpose of federation is not the power of large nations but security for citizens of all nations and for their different cultures.

The second of these general considerations tells strongly against any plan of constituting a federal authority by nomination from national governments. Whatever provision were made for giving federal representatives a tenure independent of their nominators or securing that they should represent not simply the national party in power but all parties in fair proportion, it is difficult to believe that nominated federal representatives would ever have the authority that they will need. They cannot get this authority otherwise than directly from the people whom in common affairs they will govern. Whatever the difficulties of direct election, it seems essential that they should be overcome. Nor is there reason to suppose that they cannot be overcome, if the States for inclusion are chosen with this in mind.

This means, not only that the area of the federation must be manageable, but that every member State must be a democracy, with effective provision for peaceful change of governments and policies and for free discussion and association in parties. Requirement of democracy as a condition of federal membership results, not from abstract preference of democracy to dictatorship as a means of government, but from practical reasons. The working of a federal legislature as a super-national authority would become impossible if all the representatives of a particular nation were the nominees of one man in it: very rapidly it would become a cock-pit for national interests. Again, if it becomes impossible in any member State for the national government to be changed except by violence, the federal authority controlling the armed forces may be driven to an insoluble dilemma, between allowing disorder within the federation and supporting a dictator against a probable majority of his nationals. Effective democracy is a condition of federation.

These arguments point to a federal constitution on the following lines:

(*a*) A Federal Legislature of two Houses, one with membership based on population or electorate and chosen directly by the citizens, and one with equal or nearly equal representation of the separate States, whose mem-

Peace by Federation?

bers might be either elected or nominated by the national governments.

(*b*) A Federal Executive responsible to the Federal Legislature.

(*c*) A Federal Judicature interpreting a written constitution.

(*d*) Constitutional guarantees for the maintenance of effective democracy in each of the member States, i.e. for peaceful change of governments and policies in them by free discussion and association and secret voting.

These are the main lines only. To discuss all the constitutional problems of federation and the alternatives available for their solution would occupy many books, not part of a single paper. The relations of the two Houses and possibility of deadlock between them, the methods of constituting the executive, the degree of responsibility of the federal authority for internal as well as external order, the delimitation of powers in respect of taxation or making treaties, the form in which the liberties essential to democracy shall be guaranteed in the constitution and the methods for making such guarantees effective, the provision for constitutional amendments—these and many other major problems arise as soon as federation becomes a practical issue. It is sufficient here to point out that federalism under a written constitution is not an uncharted field. Unfamiliar in Britain, its problems have been the subject of intense study and practical experiment for generations elsewhere. The problems have proved capable of solution, as they arose,

The Deeper Causes of the War

in the existing federations. There is no reason to think of them as insoluble in a new federation.

FEDERALISM BY GENERAL APPROACH

The project of international federation set out above is based on a special approach to a particular manifestation of world disorder. It may be illustrated and supported by general considerations. How can the citizen obtain peace —security from external aggression as in any settled society he has security within his State? How can justice in place of war be established as the arbiter among nations?

One negative answer to the first question is clear and points to the positive answer of federation. The individual citizen cannot obtain security against external aggression by action limited to his own State. He cannot obtain peace from his fellow-citizens: he must seek it abroad. He cannot, it may be added, obtain peace from those who are already his friends abroad by turning alliance into union: peace must be won by going into the house of one's enemy and turning him into a friend. This is a special point leading to the particular federation proposed above—a union of belligerents. The main point is that the individual citizen can get internal order within his State, but must seek external order outside, by agreement with the individuals of other nations. He must have two governments: one for his internal national affairs, one for the common affair of securing peace with

Peace by Federation?

justice between men of his nation and those of other nations. That is federalism: for each citizen two governments, with a division of powers between them prescribed by a written constitution. The individual citizen can no longer be content to set up a national government and trust to that government either to defend him by its own strength, or to part with enough of its authority to a League of Nations that will defend him at need by collective strength. The national governments once having full sovereignty do not in practice part with it; they neither like to do so, nor feel justified in doing so, for they are trustees for their own nationals. The individual citizen, if he wants effective super-national government for world order, as well as a national government for internal order, must secure that the powers of government are divided from the start. Division of powers is federalism.

The answer to the second question points the same way. How can justice be established in place of war as the arbiter among nations, so as to secure the pacific settlement of international disputes? The obvious first step in answering that question is to ask how the same end is achieved in relation to individual disputes. The answer is that it is achieved, on the one hand, by reducing the force which any individual can control to insignificance as compared with the force at the back of justice, and, on the other hand, by establishing courts to say where justice lies.

In unsettled societies the individual relies upon his

The Deeper Causes of the War

own strength for his security: each pioneer carries his musket. At a later stage he may supplement this by arrangements with particular neighbours for mutual defence. Later still comes the standing arrangement by which all members of a community agree beforehand to use their personal force in defence of any one of them and in punishment of a wrong-doer. Last of all comes the organisation of a permanent police force belonging to no individual and acting only on communal authority. Provision for individual security passes through four stages of self-defence, alliance, hue and cry, and the policeman; only with the last stage does security become assured; it is in practice assured most completely where the individual is disarmed most completely in favour of the State, while just dealing by the State itself is enforced by democracy.

Till twenty years ago, provision for the security of nations had not passed beyond the first or second stage: each nation relied on its own arms or sought to supplement them by alliance with particular neighbours. The failure of these methods is patent. Peace with justice among nations cannot be secured by the nations arming themselves or joining their arms in alliance with those of others. This is partly because the line between defensive and offensive armaments is unreal: the British Navy looks like a sure shield to the British, but looks a very different weapon to any other nation. It follows even more from inequalities in the size and strength of nations. The differences of strength between large and small

Peace by Federation?

nations are far greater than those between individuals or families. The unrestricted right of national armament to-day is patently inconsistent with small nations having any rights at all.

Peaceful settlement by justice of all disputes between nations can be made certain only on the same terms as those on which it is made certain among individuals, by making it impossible for any nation to challenge with any hope the force which justice automatically has at its command. This was the intention of the League of Nations Covenant. The war of 1914–18 led to a first experiment of adapting to international relations the device of hue and cry—the third stage in making security for the citizen. The Covenant of the League of Nations was designed, among other things, to provide collective security based on the armaments of individual nations. The failure of this experiment also is patent. The security of nations is less than ever; the assertion of national might as national right can never have been franker or more abandoned. This does not mean that the experiment of 1919 was not worth trying, or that any stronger measures would then have been accepted by the nations concerned. But it does suggest that a Covenant on the lines of that adopted in 1919 did not and probably cannot provide justice with force of the kind required, if justice is to rule among nations.

In the first place, the authors of the Covenant believed unduly in the compelling power upon nations of opinions among other nations. They spoke of public opinion as a force greater than any armaments." By far the strongest weapon we have is the weapon of public opinion." "What we rely upon is public opinion . . . and if we are wrong about it, then the whole thing is wrong."[1] On certain occasions, in the early days of the League, public opinion proved far from ineffective. But events have shown that it is not strong enough to be the strongest weapon of international order. "The scales of Justice are vain without her sword."[2]

In the second place, though the Covenant did not formally limit itself to public opinion as the force behind international justice, but contemplated more material sanctions, it relied upon individual nations to provide force for these sanctions by their own free will and from their national resources. This had three bad consequences:

(1) The power at the command of justice could not be great without making great also the power that might challenge justice. Potential wrong-doers had to provide the weapons for police-work.

(2) The policies of disarmament and of collective security came into conflict. Any of the major Powers—Britain or another—which implemented the fourth of the Fourteen Points and reduced its armaments to "the

---

[1] For those quotations from speeches by Lord Cecil (in 1919 and 1920) I am indebted to Professor E. H. Carr's recent volume *The Twenty Years' Crisis*. It should be added that these quotations by no means represent the whole of Lord Cecil's attitude. He has been a consistent advocate of further sanctions when needed.

[2] Mr. Winston Churchill in *Step by Step*, p. 38.

Peace by Federation?

lowest level consistent with domestic safety" unfitted itself thereby to be the sword of justice.

(3) The claims of justice and national policies of States supplying force came into conflict. No State would provide its national force to enforce a decision contrary to its own interests or in a way involving it in a war unpopular with its own nationals. And war as such was highly unpopular with the peoples of the States most devoted to the League of Nations.

Each of these weaknesses in turn has been illustrated in the last twenty years. It is hard to escape the conclusions drawn by Professor Carr, as to the nature of international power and the conditions of international government.

Power is an indispensable instrument of government. To internationalise government in any real sense means to internationalise power; and since independent power is the basis of the nation-state, the internationalisation of power is really a contradiction in terms.

Any real international government is impossible so long as power, which is an essential condition of government, is organised nationally.[1]

The moral drawn here, though it does not appear to be drawn by Professor Carr himself, seems equally beyond question. Enforcement of justice by hue and cry, long abandoned as a means to internal order among citizens, is even less hopeful as a means of enforcing order among

[1] *The Twenty Years' Crisis*, pp. 137, 139.

nations. To make war between nations impossible there is needed not an inter-national force, but a super-national force. Nations which really mean never to be at war again with one another, but are neither linked by indissoluble ties of blood or sympathy nor separated by unbridgeable distance, must pool their arms in federation.

Federation comes when communities recognise a common interest for which it seems worth while to sacrifice something of their freedom to be separate. To-day, in all material respects, the most distant countries named above for federation are closer than England and Scotland were at the time of their union, when it took ten or twelve days to journey from London to Edinburgh; when there was little trade, no telegraph, no broadcasting, no cycle of world depressions. To-day the common interest of these and other countries in the preservation of peace is overwhelming.

THE LIMITS OF FEDERALISM

Federation has been proposed above for a limited area. Limitation of area is essential; federalism is a strong remedy for a virulent disorder; it is not a healing lotion that can be sprayed over the world. World federation is for the millennium. The federation projected here is for the next peace treaty: it is a federation of nations which from fresh experience of war will be determined to make as certain as they can that war will never be repeated.

If, in addition to the nations already named for

Peace by Federation?

inclusion, the United States of America desired to enter a Peace Federation, that would be a welcome revolutionary fact leading to readjustment of all plans. But that is too much to hope for and not necessary to the project here in view. World order, as distinct from European order, cannot be established without the co-operation of the United States of America. But the co-operation can take a form less intimate than federation with European States.

As regards the rest of Europe, the requirement of effective national democracy as a condition of federation, would exclude automatically nearly the whole of it: Russia, Italy, Turkey, Spain, Portugal, and most of the Balkan States have Governments substantially autocratic.

The inclusion of Germany herself in the federation depends upon her return to democracy. There is no reason to think this unlikely if, with Hitlerism defeated, the democracies act promptly to keep Stalinism at bay. There is no reason, either, for democrats to be half-hearted in assertion of their principle. The doctrine of 1919 that making the world safe for democracy was the way to make it safe for all mankind was sound doctrine and remains so: the bitter laugh to-day is against those who derided it. The view that it is no concern of other nations what kind of government there is in Germany is academic theorising divorced from fact. If at the end of this war Germany cannot become democratic, the other nations of Europe will need to make themselves secure by military domination without partnership.

The Deeper Causes of the War

But there is no need to press democracy upon nations other than Germany. Their present Governments may be those which fit their present needs. They should not be tempted to change for the sake of joining the federation of Western democracies. Some of them may wish to form a different federation of their own, corresponding to their interests. The constitution of the Peace Federation would provide for accessions, but would not give a right of accession to any State that could satisfy formal requirements. Admission would depend upon the consent of the federation; and that consent might well be refused. A federation of north-western Europe and the British Dominions is manageable; once established it might be expected to grow in unity. Inclusion of other European countries, with different standards of life and with little or no experience of democracy, would weaken the federation and might end in revival of nationalist manœuvres.

To some friends of federalism the suggestion that the area of federation must be limited strikes a chilling note. To some critics it appears a convenient handle for attack. The critics see in a selective federation an attack upon some other nation or some ideology. The friends feel that selection destroys the liberating virtue of a principle. The answer to friends and critics is the same, and in two stages. First, the boundaries suggested here for the Peace Federation are neither absolute nor final. They are those which, having regard to present conditions and prospective attitudes at the end of this war, seem most likely

Peace by Federation?

both to bring a federation into being and to enable it to function. Later revolutions in the minds of men may open the way to larger groupings. Second, some limitation of area, so far from taking the virtue out of the federal idea, is of its essence. Federalism is a principle which can be shared by all. A federation of nations is not a principle but a partnership. It is a partnership moreover of an active kind. Its analogy is not the co-operative store which any consumer who pays the subscription may join and which is strengthened by every new consumer. Its analogy is the co-operation of those who work together in a common task—of college or factory or family. Each working partnership must be based on compatibilities and must be selective for its purpose. But partnership is not exclusive. The closest partnership known—that of marriage—does not bar all other relations, with individuals or with other partnerships; those who enter this partnership do not thereby declare hostility to the rest of the human race.

Unquestionably any prospect of such a federation as that here projected would cause perturbation in some quarters, and raise questions for many peoples. Russia would see in it the end of her present adventures and in due course the loss of anything she might have gained. Italy would see in it a barrier to aspirations which she regards as legitimate. The United States and many other countries would be interested in its treatment of dependencies and in its economic policies.

It may be presumed that the federation itself will be

The Deeper Causes of the War

peaceable. It will be too strong to fear attack from any other power, and will thus have no temptation to organise defensive war; it will have no reason to be jealous of voluntary association of other States or of full federation between them. It will be too varied in interests to be aggressive; it will have pacifism in its bones and disarmament as a natural goal. But the federation will have to be much more than peaceable in itself if it is to serve fully the cause of world order. "The armed force of the Peace Federation shall be used to support justice among nations and to resist aggression wherever it may occur. The armed force of the Peace Federation shall not be used to gain for all or any of its members territory or economic advantage over any other state." Declarations of this nature, though they could hardly be written into the constitution of the federation, should be deeply engraved in its policies from the start.

First, the federation should be prepared to use its armed forces in support of international justice throughout the world. In Europe no more than its own force would be needed. Outside Europe there is another focus of disorder—in Japan, China and Asiatic Russia. Here the federation could not act alone, but should be prepared to act for the restoration of order, in collaboration with the United States of America.

Second, as the federation should support justice against force throughout the world, so it should be prepared to accept justice in governing its own relation to other states. The federation will be acutely conscious of its own

Peace by Federation?

good faith and good intentions, but they may not always be obvious to others. It will not be easy for an immensely powerful association always to agree with others where justice lies, in its own cause. The acid test is likely to come over the treatment of dependencies in relation to the trading interests of other States.

For both the purposes named—to guide the use of the federation's force in maintaining international justice, and to allow the federation itself to accept justice in its own cause in place of its own decisions—there is need for international machinery. Justice needs her scales as well as her sword. Without something in the nature of a World Council open to every State which recognises the interests of other States, without something in the nature of an Equity Tribunal, the Peace Federation outlined here cannot render its full service to the cause of world order. How these general organs of world order should be established and governed, how they should be related to existing institutions, how far they can be built on existing institutions, are themes for another discussion. But in one form or other they would surely be established if once the heart of Europe were healed and healthy.

The Peace Federation projected here is limited in area, so that it may be strong and real. The services which it may render to world order are not limited.

First, the federation can guarantee, as nothing else can, peace with justice within its area.

Second, the federation by its own strength can guarantee peace with justice in Europe. It is unlikely itself to be guilty of aggression, based as it will be on so many deeply pacific peoples with so great a variety of individual interests. It will be far too strong to be challenged by any European Power or any combination of such Powers. It can and should be prepared to guarantee the just rights of all the other nations in Europe, individually or grouped in federations.

Third, with peace in Europe guaranteed, it will be in a position to collaborate on equal terms with the peace-loving nations of America, in spreading peace with justice in the one part of the world that may still be a source of war and aggression, in the Far East to Europe and beyond the Far West of the United States.

THE NEXT STEP

A federation of the present belligerents and neighbour neutrals, if once it were established, might lead to peace with justice for all mankind. What is the chance of establishing it? On what does realisation of this dream of an ordered, secure, progressive world depend? On two things and two alone. The first condition is the defeat of Hitlerism in Germany—exorcism of the foul fiend that now possesses a great people. The second condition is that when Hitlerism has been exorcised, the people concerned—Britain, France and Germany first and others following them—should be willing to take those steps towards federal co-operation and limitation of national sovereignty which alone can secure them against return of war.

Peace by Federation?

Will these two conditions in their turn be satisfied? No one to-day can answer that question. No one can say just in what circumstances the chance of making peace will come; with what balance of strength between the belligerents and with what parties to the war. The solid ground beneath our feet is being shaken by great forces. The coming year may hold events shattering to optimism; it may hold events that will make pessimism to-day look like shameful cowardice to-morrow.

But it is not only the future that is dark. No one can say to-day what is in the thoughts of the German people —those who to many in this country were once the most sympathetic and friendly nation other than our own. The hearts of these millions of human beings are dark to us. They cannot speak to us; we hear nothing but the braying of their masters. They cannot hear us, except by stealth. All that we know is that when last we were in communion with the German people, in September 1938, we thought that we recognised, in their acclamation of the delusive settlement at Munich, a peaceful spirit to match our own, and a desire equal to our own to avoid the horror and the shame of war.

Whether we were right or wrong, the deafening of German ears is not so complete as the gag upon their voices; though we cannot hear them at all, it is not wholly impossible for them to hear us. It is worth our while therefore to avoid saying those things which cannot but strengthen them in desperate support of their present rulers. They are being told that their troubles

The Deeper Causes of the War

before the new war were due to the injustice of the Allies at Versailles; that the Allies, if victorious, will impose conditions yet more shameful than those of Versailles; that the very existence of the German people is at stake. In so far as they believe this, we strengthen their belief by talk of destroying the unity of Germany, by talk of such terms of peace as we should never accept for ourselves while we had a man left to fight or a gun to fire. What we ought to say to them is rather this: "*If and so long as you support the claim of your rulers that German might is the sole measure of German right, then the fight must continue until you change your minds; the tangible evidence of changed minds will be abandonment of the conquests which you have just made by force in Poland and in Czecho-Slovakia, and the giving of freedom to Austria to decide her own fate. If, however, you are already of that better mind, if you cause us to believe, as we should like to believe, that you are content to live in your own lands as we do in ours, respecting the rights of other nations, then we are ready to confer with you as to the means by which together you and we can meet three common needs. The first is the need to make war between you and ourselves impossible for ever; our plan is to pool your arms and ours in federation; if you have another plan as effective for the purpose we will consider it. The second is the need to deprive you of all sense of injustice; our plan is that you with others should share with us those economic advantages in colonial lands which you think are unfairly ours. The third is the need to increase the prosperity and security of your lives and ours; our plan*

Peace by Federation?

is to join with you and others in seeking solutions of the common economic problems of mankind. One thing more we have to say. *We mean that this time the war shall end when it does end; there shall be nothing again of what you have been taught to call the blockade which followed the Armistice of* 1918; *once you have repaired the damage of your recent conquests, there shall be no reparations. On the day that fighting stops there shall, if we have our way, come into action an International Reconstruction Commission charged with the duties of relieving distress, repairing war damages and re-establishing prosperity for all at the common charge of all. We hope to forge in that the first link of our lasting equal union."*

That is what we should try to say to the German people. In the view of the British people the peace for which they are fighting is a peace of fair-play for citizens of all nations; it is a peace against which the German people would not wish to fight, if they understood it. To persuade the German people of this is the only short cut to end the war—the charm which might save millions of lives.

But the channels of persuasion are nearly blocked. The hearts of the German people are dark to us and their ears are all but closed. To those who are not belligerents, and to our allies and ourselves, we can speak. As regards the neutrals, it is worth while to persuade them that whatever may be our success in the war, we desire and will take nothing from success but a gain that we can share equally with all mankind—peace with justice in an ordered world; that ending this war we shall be prepared to unite with them and others in constructive tasks of peace. If the greatest of the neutral nations should come to feel that, in this age of brigand empires and oppression of the weak, it is good to have a giant's strength, but wrong to keep a giant's strength locked up for self-defence, then that nation would become, as she is not yet, the Hope of the World; man's struggle for freedom would be shortened; hundreds of thousands of the youth of all nations now in conflict would live, who otherwise in the next years will die.

To our allies we can speak with the frankness of indissoluble friendship. The French see some things more clearly than the British do; the British see some things more clearly than the French do; true perspective needs a combination of views from different angles. Whatever our allies think, we want to know. What we say to ourselves, we say to them.

Among ourselves our task is by free discussion to fill in, line by line, a picture of the world that we should like to see after the war. By discussion we may convince ourselves that the world, if we take the right steps, can be a world without war. That in itself would be a potent aid to realising the first condition of this dream —to success in the present war. For success will depend first and foremost upon maintaining the spirit of the common people in France and in the British Commonwealth.

There is no doubt of the determination with which

Peace by Federation?

the British, in Britain and overseas, have turned from passionate desire for peace to acceptance of war. The final words of the Prime Minister's speech in announcing war could not be bettered as a statement of the feeling which has led us to this point; we have set out to fight what appear to us evil things—"brute force, bad faith, injustice, oppression and persecution." But while a negative reason of fighting evil may be sufficient for the beginning of a war, something else may be needed when determination comes to be tested by tribulation, by exhaustion, by fears of defeat. Then may be required the hope that at the end of war, not merely will evil be destroyed, but something good, something worth dying for and worth killing for, will be established. Only that hope sustained us from the frustration of 1916 to the victory of 1918. Only that hope can bring us with certainty to the same opportunity again. During this war, as early as we can, we must make a positive plan for the world that is to follow the war. The negative virtue of hating Hitlerism does not suffice.

Our plan for the world must be positive; it must also be new. The defeat of the high expectation of 1919, that war was finally banished from the world, was shattering and has left many even of those who go without question to-day to fight, without the hope which inspired those who fought a generation ago. They can and should be made to hope: the fact that the world failed once is not a reason for assuming that it will fail again in finding the way to end war. But hope will not return to the spell of

The Deeper Causes of the War

old catchwords and general phrases. We must convince ourselves, old and young, that we have both a positive plan and a new plan.

Finally, the plan must be one that commends itself to the willing acceptance of our people and the others concerned. There can be no reasonable doubt that such a plan as that outlined above could work if it had the support of the peoples for whom it was established. Neither that nor any other scheme for world order can work which has not that support. Federation across national boundaries is both a positive plan and a new plan. All that remains is to see whether it is a plan that commends itself to the nations.

The title of this paper is a question: Peace by Federation? The mark of interrogation does not imply doubt that the federation here proposed, if once it were established by the wishes of the peoples concerned, would bring lasting peace to them, and lay the foundations of peace throughout the world; the federation would grow in unity and strength, solving each practical problem as it arose. The mark of interrogation stands because there are two other questions to which the answer is less certain. Will the peoples concerned be prepared to accept a plan of this kind? Is there any other plan which they would accept that would be as likely to achieve order in the world? The answer to the second question in my view is probably but not certainly "No." The answer to the first question, in my view, is probably but not certainly "Yes." I believe that

Peace by Federation?

when the issue is raised the peoples concerned will be prepared to barter arms for security and sovereignty for civilisation.

But there is no way of answering this question finally except by asking it and inviting discussion among the people themselves. Federation of kindred nations will work if they desire it. It will not work as a plan thrust on them by their rulers. To persuade the people of this country and of her allies and of other countries to choose this plan for themselves is the object of this paper. That is the next step.

Federation across national boundaries is a plan so new that it will be rejected by some critics as Utopian. If by Utopian these critics mean to describe a plan based on desires divorced from realities, then the plan is not Utopian. Whether the project outlined here be right or wrong, it starts from reality. It is based on facts: on the general fact of secular changes in the scientific and material equipment of mankind, making out of date old tribal groupings and isolations; upon two special revolutionary facts—of the unification of Germany and of aggressive Communism in Russia. These facts between them have changed the conditions of peace in Europe and the forms of government required there.

If, on the other hand, the term Utopian implies the vision of a world different from the world we live in, then the term describes literally the proposal of this paper. The plan of this paper is Utopian, for it aims at making a world different from the world that we have

The Deeper Causes of the War

known for nearly a generation. The plan dares and needs to be Utopian because the choice is no longer between Utopia and the pleasant, ordered world that our fathers knew. The choice is between Utopia and Hell.